BORN TO BACKSLIDE

A DIVINE STRUGGLE

ANDY KONIGSMARK

APOCRYPHILE
PRESS

Apocryphile Press
1700 Shattuck Ave #81
Berkeley, CA 94709
www.apocryphilepress.com

Copyright © 2020 by Andy Konsigsmark
Printed in the United States of America
ISBN 978-1-949643-66-4 | paperback
ISBN 978-1-949643-67-1 | ePub

CONTENTS

INTRODUCTION

To all of my readers, this book reflects the roller coaster of life. It follows a wayward evangelical Christian who marches towards adulthood. Along the way, we will laugh, cry, and contemplate life together.

I have tried to the best of my ability to recreate the events, locales and conversations from my memories. In order to maintain anonymity and protect unspoken prayer requests, some names and places have been changed to protect the guilty. Additionally, some identifying characteristics and details such as physical properties, occupations and places of residence have been changed as well.

Together, we will explore some of the most painful and exhilarating moments in life. Along the way, I encountered numerous stop signs, but the show must go on. This collection of stories serves as a reminder that the struggle is what makes life beautiful.

CHAPTER 1

ALL EYES ON THE GLADIATOR

"I asked God for a bike, but I know God doesn't work that way. So, I stole a bike and asked for forgiveness."—Emo Williams

WILL JESUS HELP YOU WIN?

It was November of 2007. Within minutes, I would be hoisted onto a twenty-foot platform to compete on the TV show *American Gladiators* hosted by Hulk Hogan. As the production team was making last-minute safety gear adjustments, one of the producers asked, "Andy, do you think you're going to win because you're a Christian?"

"No, I do not think I'm going to win because I'm a Christian."

Determined to land the perfect media soundbite, he continued, "Andy, will you pray to Jesus for the strength to win?"

From a production standpoint, a brash youth minister calling upon the faith of Jesus to win a game show is great television. The questions were ridiculous, and an insult to the Christian faith.

"No, I will not ask Jesus for the strength to win. He doesn't care whether I win or lose a game show. Therefore, I'm not going to waste His time with petty prayers. I will pray for God to be glorified. I will pray for the safety and protection of my fellow competitors. I will pray for the tenacity of the gladiators. But I will not pray for victory. In case you missed the first sound bite, let me say it again—Jesus does not have skin in this game."

The production team was not impressed by my bold comments. A trash-talking evangelical asking Jesus for victory creates binge-worthy television. Despite their best-laid plans, however, I had zero desire to be portrayed as a polarizing Christian personality on national television. I am not ashamed of my faith, but trying to use Jesus as a secret weapon is pure ignorance. Jesus is my savior, not my four-leaf clover.

BACK UP A MINUTE

How did I get to this point? In August of 2007, I was a twenty-nine-year-old graduate student living in Pasadena, California. Two years earlier, I had left the serenity of Sun Valley, Idaho, to pursue a Master of Divinity through Fuller Seminary. Outside of class, I was working for a local catering company, hustling for tips, sleeping in bunkbeds to save money, and perfecting my craft as a stand-up comic. Becoming a competitor on *American Gladiators* was not even on the radar.

Then, one phone call from my sister changed the trajectory of my life.

"Andy, I just saw a commercial on NBC saying they're holding open auditions for *Last Comic Standing*. You owe it to yourself to audition. This could be your big break!"

Moments after hanging up, I logged onto the NBC website. After scrolling through several links, I learned casting for the next season of *Last Comic* Standing would take place in the spring of 2008. With auditions on hold, my dreams of becoming a working comedian would have to wait for another couple of months. In the meantime, the production team encouraged all interested comics to submit audition videos and sign up for email updates.

Before logging off, I was sidetracked by a casting link for the *New American Gladiators* with Hulk Hogan. After a twenty-year hiatus, NBC was bringing spandex back to Prime Time. I couldn't believe what I was reading. One of my favorite childhood television shows was making a comeback.

Just minutes earlier, I was an aspiring comic. Now, with a single button tap, I was registering for the chance to become a competitor on *New American Gladiators*. In less than twenty-four hours, NBC was holding an open casting call at Gold's Gym in Venice Beach. I was certain the parking lot would be filled with hundreds of men and women with gladiator aspirations.

At the crack of dawn, I hopped into my truck to make the forty-minute drive to Venice Beach. When I arrived, I was shocked by the scene surrounding the gym. An hour before sunrise, not hundreds but *thousands* of aspiring gladiators were anxiously forming audition lines. The crowd was brimming with athletes of all shapes, sizes, and ability levels. The scene was reminiscent of a pack of wild gorillas who felt the need to beat their chests every few minutes to remind everyone who was still king.

I waited in line for over seven hours, making idle chit-chat with bodybuilders, personal trainers, professional athletes, and a couple of hungover college students. While waiting for their audition numbers to be called, the restless crowd told endless stories of athletic greatness. The long wait would end with a three-minute audition to impress the casting team.

"Number 1572. Number 1572."

Finally, my number was being called. Within seconds, I grabbed the pull-up bar to start the fitness test. Running on an empty stomach, I impressed myself by pumping out twenty-five strict pull-ups in under a minute. I felt confident with my initial results until I heard that a forty-nine-year-old female Marine had cranked out forty-two!

Dropping from the bar, I defiantly blasted out fifty chest-to-floor push-ups. Rising to my feet, I sprinted to the finish line to complete the forty-yard dash. Panting for breath, I was hustled by the production team into a small tent to take a few photos and answer some questions.

A disinterested casting assistant looked down at his clipboard, "William, your application says you've had reconstructive surgeries on both knees to repair torn anterior cruciate ligaments. These are major injuries. Do you think you'll be able to compete with other competitors who've never been injured as severely?"

"For the record," I replied, "my first name is William, but everyone calls me Andy. As for my knees, they feel good. During physical therapy, I pushed my body to the limits. After tearing my ACL for the first time at nineteen, I refused to let a major injury put an end to my athletic pursuits. We all fall sometimes, but it's how we rise to our feet that people remember."

"Thanks, Andy. Do you have any other cliché lines you would like to share? Maybe you want to tell us you'll give it one hundred and ten percent, or maybe that this is your Cinderella story."

Ignoring the snide comments, I looked into the camera, waiting for the next question.

"For this installment of American Gladiators, we're looking for individuals who are more than great athletes; we want people with great stories. Would you mind telling us the most difficult thing in your life that you've had to overcome?"

I thought for a moment. "At the age of six, I was labeled as mentally handicapped. I had to be removed from the traditional classroom and placed in special ed. My parents were told I would be lucky to graduate high school. Despite these labels, I did graduate. I also graduated college with honors. Now I'm working on a master's degree."

With a deadpan expression, the casting assistant replied, "Okay, thanks for that heartwarming story. Just one more question. Andy, what do you do for a living?"

As a side note, I hate this question. Few people can truly be defined by their occupation. For example, my father wanted to be a pilot, but he didn't have perfect eyesight so he became a mortgage lender for thirty years instead, and never enjoyed clocking in at eight a.m. every day. The job was not exciting or interesting to him, but it provided his family with safety and security. It also came with great benefits and solid pay, but home loans do not fill the dreams of five-year-old boys. Our father was a valuable employee who never missed a day of work, but his lifelong profession had little to do with his character, the young man who dreamed of soaring where angels dwell. My father is more than a banker who made a living buying and selling home loans, but even that second choice profession didn't dim his spirit. Away from the office, he embraced life as a generous, fun-loving, adventurous storyteller.

"I'm studying to be a minister," I finally blurted. This must have been the magic answer. Auditions for competition television shows are more than physical tests. Casting directors are searching for individuals with intriguing stories or outrageous personalities, not just elite athletes. To boost ratings, they need competitive athletes with compelling stories, because American television audiences desire more than vanilla ice cream. They're looking for individuals with rocky road personalities with some Texas Pete Hot Sauce on the side.

WHAT HAPPENED NEXT?

Two weeks after auditioning to become a competitor on the *New American Gladiators*, I received a phone call from the casting directors. After auditioning 20,000 prospective athletes, they had decided I was moving on to the second round of casting. To move forward in the process, the production team needed a five-minute video depicting my life as a seminary student.

The short film captured a behind-the-scenes viewpoint of a financially challenged graduate student. It focused on the odd assortment of thrift store furniture inside our rent-controlled apartment. I dedicated a precious thirty seconds to the bunkbeds I shared with another male student. To capture the producers' attention, I recorded moments from a New Testament Theology class, images of my wrecked Ford truck, and one painful moment stumbling over Spanish as I purchased *Oreos* at the local supermercado.

A month after submitting the award-winning video, forty contenders, including myself, were invited to compete for twenty-four spots on the upcoming show. At Sony Studios, located in Culver City, hopeful, modern-day gladiators were given five days to display their athletic talents and personalities. During this period, we had the opportunity to train for several events, including Hang Tough, Joust, and The Pyramid. But no amount of training could fully prepare anyone to be chased by a gladiator in front of a live television audience.

Before practicing each event, producers would say, "Competitors, do not go one hundred percent. We don't want anyone to get hurt before we begin filming. Please keep your effort levels closer to fifty percent."

How in the world can anyone judge fifty percent of their effort level? For competitive athletes, it's impossible to compete with one another at fifty percent; there is an on switch and an off switch. A medium switch does not exist. Telling an athlete to hold back on the reigns is akin to telling a kindergarten student to eat half of a candy bar. Of course, the poor kid is going to devour the entire Snickers! The non-athletic production team did not understand the genetic makeup of competitive athletes. During one of the training sessions, competitors were randomly assigned partners to practice wrestling for one of the show's new events called *Tilt*—a blend of tug-of-war and wrestling while balancing on unstable platforms. Unfortunately, these platforms were not yet ready, so the production team threw some hard mats on the floor and encouraged improperly-trained competitors to use them for wrestling practice instead.

Due to a stroke of bad luck, I was tasked with wrestling a mild-mannered Mormon named Jackson. This young father of two did not carry the swagger of the other athletes, but as the saying goes, looks can be deceiving. Jackson was an All-American wrestler in college and one of the most incredible athletes I have ever encountered. The dude could do a standing double-backflip before it was even thought humanly possible.

Minutes after hitting the mats with Captain Backflip, I was fighting with all of my might to avoid being pinned. Action Jackson was using every skill possible to dominate the match. I, on the other hand, had zero firsthand experience with wrestling, grappling or martial arts. I was just a Bible-thumping nerd who loved snowboarding and lifting weights. From the outset, the plan went bad. I had two options—fight for my life or succumb to Jackson's dominant wrestling techniques.

Despite being the supreme underdog, I opted to fight until the bitter end. Jackson might win, but I was determined not to fold like a lounge chair. Seconds after the match began, Jackson drove his shoulder into my chest and began working my body into a pretzel formation. To maintain any level of respect and prove I deserved to be a competitor on *American Gladiators,* it was imperative that I muster every ounce of strength I possessed and put up some kind of a fight.

Laying helpless on my back, Jackson began pressing his full weight into my chest with his shoulder, forcing the air out of my lungs. Tunnel vision was beginning to set in. If I didn't fight back, this wrestling match would be over in a matter of seconds. My head was pounding like a jackhammer, and my heart was racing like a Ferrari on the Autobahn.

Moments before passing out from complete exhaustion, the production team mercifully stopped the match. My prayers were answered when a production assistant began yelling, "Alright, alright! Break it up! Break it up, you guys! I thought we told you to go fifty percent!"

I had the impulse to tell him it's impossible to wrestle at half speed if you're trying to win, but I bit my tongue to avoid getting booted from the show for insubordination.

As I was struggling to my feet and fighting to catch my breath, I noticed Jackson's face was filled with pain. I wondered what was wrong. There was no way I could have hurt the guy. He dominated the match from the moment we hit the mats. He was in total control, while I flopped around like an earthworm on hot asphalt. I spent the entire match in survival mode, thinking, "Slow down your breathing. Slow it down."

The onsite medical team gathered around Jackson to examine any injuries he may have incurred during the match. Watching the scene unfold, I began to notice a slight throbbing sensation in my right shoulder. Playing sports over the years, I have been injured numerous times. As the pain was radiating, I was certain it was nothing serious. But as my adrenaline level began to return to normal, the throbbing sensation rapidly became a debilitating pain.

A short time later, we were loaded into a production van for an emergency room field trip. After taking x-rays and meeting with doctors, it was determined that Jackson had broken his wrist. He believed the injury occurred during an attempt to finish the match with a cross-face cradle. In an effort to pin my shoulders to the mat, Jackson locked his arms around my face, and as they tightened around my jaw, I drove my legs forward, attempting a reversal, which flipped the two of us onto our backs. His wrist became trapped underneath our bodies during the flip. Jackson's journey to become an American Gladiator was over. The humble father from Utah left the hospital with his wrist in a cast. No surgery was required, but his wrist would be immobilized for a minimum of six weeks.

Upon further examination, an emergency room doctor diagnosed my injury as a torn shoulder labrum. Without undergoing an MRI, the full extent of the damage was unknown. A doctor injected my shoulder with a cortisone shot to reduce the swelling. Then a steroid injection was delivered to jumpstart the healing process. I was told if the pain didn't subside after a month, I should schedule a follow-up appointment with an orthopedic surgeon. As I was signing all of the paperwork and forking over money I did not have, the doctor said, "Mr. Konigsmark, it is my professional opinion that you should withdraw from competing on this television show. Your long-term health is more important than competing for money."

Re-playing the doctor's words, I thought to myself, "Fat chance, Bucko! This might be my only opportunity to become a gladiator."

On the ride back to our hotel, Jackson must have noticed the guilt written across my face. His words were drenched with compassion, "You put up a great fight. It wasn't your fault I broke my wrist. It's just one of things that happens when you compete. When the show finally airs, I'll tell my kids, 'That's the minister who broke my wrist.'"

THE FINAL DAY

On the last day of training, the remaining thirty-nine competitors and I were gathered in a room to learn our fates. Twenty-four of us would be selected to compete on the show. In addition, four people would be selected as alternates. The alternates were scheduled to remain on call if one of our fellow competitors was injured during filming. Based on rough math, eleven unfortunate finalists would be going home without receiving participation medals, orange slices, or juice boxes from the team mom.

I listened in total disbelief as my name had been omitted from the list of twelve men who were selected to compete on the show. The production team must have made a mistake. I had done everything possible to ensure a chance to compete. I did not want to be an alternate, but it was better than nothing. A few minutes later, I learned my fate. After coming this far in the casting process, I was unworthy to be an alternate. Ouch! I wasn't even good enough to be second string.

As I was preparing to take the walk of shame home, an unexpected event happened. A couple of male competitors from New York, both named Tony, starting throwing haymakers at each other. To this day, I have no idea what they were fighting about. One minute it was, "Best pizza on the Southside is . . ." and the next it was, "Your mother makes the worst rigatoni in the Bronx." Bada-bing, bada-boom, Tony number two was sent packing. This unceremonious exit created room for an aspiring minister and comedian to join the contestant pool as an alternate.

CHAPTER 2

BORN TO BACKSLIDE

"I've done everything the Bible says—even the stuff that contradicts the other stuff!" —Ned Flanders

GROWING UP EVANGELICAL

A conservative Christian home served as the background for my childhood. Our church culture taught us that the Bible was the authority on everything. If the Bible said the earth was created in seven days, then the earth was created in seven literal days. No questions asked. No room for discussion. End of story. On Sunday mornings, our pastor would say, "The Bible teaches, I believe it. Now tithe."

Pregnant women of all faiths, creeds and colors ask God for healthy children. Fathers come seeking resources to provide for their families. Teenagers pray that their parents will not find their stash of beer hidden in the toolshed. My mother uttered a very unique prayer before I entered this world. A few months before giving birth, she watched *Saturday Night Fever* and became infatuated with John Travolta's butt chin. As I patiently developed inside her womb, my mother fervently began praying for her child to be born with a cleft chin. Her prayers were miraculously answered. Now everyone can experience the sovereign nature of God by focusing on my perfect butt chin, or chin butt, whichever you prefer.

Life began inauspiciously, including several years ripping off a dirty diaper while sprinting naked out the back door. My feet would hit the grass with a furious pace as I ran for the freedom of our chain link fence. My mother, known as The Wise Owl, would start yelling, "Stop him before he gets to the fence!"

On the best days, my fingers and toes would become enmeshed with the cool metal. Calling upon my sloth-like death-grip, I would latch on to the fence, make my entire diminutive form rigid, and start to hold my breath. At this point, however, it was too late. My mother would be forced to wait for my face to turn purple before she could begin prying my fingers loose. These diaper-less moments defined the early years of my life, but everyone in our evangelical circle knew I was born to backslide.

For our friends who exist outside the conservative evangelical realm, backsliding is when an individual turns away from God to pursue their own selfish desires. Southern Baptist Preachers love to warn their flock about the dangers of backsliding. For example, "Even after I accepted Jesus as my Lord and Savior, I couldn't stop myself from ordering the extra cocktails at the local strip club." Drinking and going to the strip club is slippery slope that will allow even the most noble of men to backslide into the pits of hell.

SEX IS A FOUR-LETTER WORD

From the day I entered this world, and for the majority of my childhood, prayer, salvation, and the fear of eternal damnation served as my life's backdrop. First Mega Southern Baptist Church rallied against abortion, homosexuality, and premarital sex. As a matter of fact, they hated anything to do with sex. If you wanted to go straight to hell, sex was the quickest path. Thou shalt not talk about sex, know about sex, or think about sex. So sayeth the Southern Baptist Convention.

Our conservative leaders at First Mega Church affirmed the supremacy of Scripture. From the pulpit, our pastor boldly proclaimed we can love God but not the world, for that was another path straight to hell. As a result, the only safe place was sitting on a pew on Sunday morning.

Sunday after Sunday, I fidgeted in my seat during the worship service. As I was squirming and drawing dirty looks from the church deacons, I heard that believing in Jesus Christ is the only way to live for eternity in heaven. Everyone who denied Jesus was going to burn in hell. As a result, saving the world from burning in hell was our mission.

Saving your heathen neighbors from hell is a difficult mission for a five-year-old boy to understand. I wanted to save our heathen neighbors, but I also wanted to play with my G.I. Joe's. Such a dilemma. Do you play with *Snake Eyes* with the Kung Fu grip, or tell your best friend he's going to hell if he doesn't change his vile ways? (I chose *Snake Eyes*.)

On a regular basis, the church told our conservative congregation the culture of the world may change, but the truth and morality of the Bible never will. If your friends are having fun, you can believe they will not be having fun for long because they are pressing the accelerator on the highway to hell. Fun was wrong, church was right, and there was no grey area in between.

In our conservative church subculture, no one questioned the authority of the Bible. It was literally written by God and put into the hands of men. It was heresy to suggest the Bible contained errors or discrepancies. The problem with this viewpoint is it turns the Bible into a house of cards that comes toppling down if a single error is discovered.

It was inconceivable to question the veracity of the senior pastor's sermons, his desire to ask the congregation for money, or his miraculous hair growth. When I was five years old, the minister's head looked like a snow globe, but by the age of twelve, we all personally witnessed his hair raise from the dead. So, if the once-balding pastor said it from the pulpit, then it must be true.

The authority of God trickled all the way down to the janitorial team. I thought peeing on the bathroom floor was just an accident, but it turned out to be an abomination against God too. If we asked the Sunday School teachers a question, we were labeled as heretics. One time, I raised the nerve to question the accuracy of elephant poop and Noah's Ark. This innocent question led to my immediate expulsion from a month-long study on the Book of Genesis.

My evangelical upbringing might sound controlling and punitive, but if you're raised in a conservative Christian subculture, this is normal. Within my circle of influence, friends and family did not attend PG-13 or R-rated movies. Parents did not drink alcohol, smoke cigarettes, or use swear words. Only sinners and degenerates listened to non-Christian music.

Divorce was also a tool of the devil. Satan loved to eat spicy hot wings at *Hooters* on Sunday afternoon. Heavy Metal music, Ouija Boards, and *Dungeons and Dragons* were dubious forms of witchcraft. *The Simpsons, 90210, and Three's Company* were television shows devised for the sole purpose of leading children into the bowels of evil.

SWEATER VESTS

I do not resent my parents for the environment in which they raised our family. Sure, we were strongly encouraged to memorize Bible verses during summer vacation. Yes, we were expected to wear sweater vests, bowties and khakis to church every Sunday morning. But our home was full of affection, love, and laughter. As one might expect, it was also free of alcohol, cigarettes, yelling, swear words, nudity, and Iron Maiden. First Mega Church encouraged parents to replace outside culture with conservative Christian values. Whenever we hopped into our station wagon, the local Christian station was blaring at full blast on the radio. On rare occasions, a Madonna or Michael Jackson album would slip through the local security checkpoint and find itself hidden in the thick shag carpet covering our entire playroom. When these moments occurred, a family meeting was called, and the album was ceremoniously melted in the oven. Some of the greatest hits of the 1980's remained at the bottom of our oven for years.

Cartoons were also painstakingly analyzed. *Looney Toons*, *The Jetsons* and *The Flintstones* were given a clean stamp of approval. Unfortunately, *The Simpsons* were unacceptable because Bart was rude to his father. *The Smurfs* was another show that did not meet church standards. Gargamel was an evil wizard intent on leading young children to start practicing witchcraft. One minute they'd be watching Smurfs innocently dancing on toadstools, and the next they would perform a midnight séance in the treehouse.

This might sound unbelievable, but I was twenty-five years old the first time I heard my father say a swear word. His favorite Christian swear words included dagnabbit, gosh-darn-it, and dang. Within the family unit, the words butt, crap and fart were treated as swear words. Washing our mouths out with soap would be a reality if we dared to utter one of these insidious words.

Imagine my complete shock when our six-year old daughter said her first R-rated word.

"Dad, I heard a bad word at school today," she said. "Can I ask you what it means?"

In my apparently naïve mind, I thought she was going to say

stupid, dumb, or ugly. Nope, right there in the kitchen, she dropped the queen mother of cuss words—the F-bomb. She then proceeded to ask what the word means.

"Sweetness, I am not entirely sure I understand the etymology of the word. Matter of fact, I'm not sure I understand the etymology of the word etymology. But, we don't use that kind of word at school, church, or in front of Nana. We don't use it toward your little brother or your parents either."

"Well, when can we use it, Dad?"

"Honey, it's not a word I care to use at all, but I imagine some people might scream this word when our beloved Georgia Bulldogs can't convert on fourth and goal in the National Championship game."

"Dad, that doesn't make sense."

"No, honey, it doesn't. The Bulldogs should have tried a quarterback sneak on third and short."

CHURCH CULTURE

First Mega Church stood at the center of our family's spiritual life. On really special Sunday mornings, when the family station wagon was being repaired by the local shade tree mechanic, all six family members would cram into my father's Volkswagen Bug to make the twenty-minute drive to church. On these joyous mornings, we would come to a screeching halt in the parking lot and begin spilling out of the car like clowns at the circus. From an early age, we sat through big church, learning about the evils of alcohol, the shame of premarital sex, the sins of homosexuality, and the dangers of backsliding into the devil's grip.

Conservative theology flowed from the pulpit into all aspects of church life. Church members would boldly proclaim, "Adam and Eve didn't come from no apes." Another favorite: "I hate bananas. Ain't that proof I didn't use to be no monkey?"

Despite advances in science, people within our church community held tightly to the belief that science stood in direct opposition to God, which seems ironic considering most evangelical parents would rush to the emergency room if their son or daughter broke an arm. I do not recall church members driving to church to ask the pastor to heal their children's broken bones or stitch up their wounds. The majority of Americans rightly run toward the science of medicine in search of healing.

For the Christians within our community, it was unthinkable to question the authenticity of biblical narratives. If the Bible says Noah gathered two of every animal upon a giant ship, then there is nothing to discuss. As an adult, I still encounter adults who insist on a literal translation of the Bible. For these individuals, it is essential to believe Jonah was swallowed by a whale, the world was destroyed by a flood, and some people lived for over eight hundred years.

In the book of Numbers, readers encounter Balaam and a talking donkey. "And the LORD opened the mouth of the donkey, and she said to Balaam, 'What have I done to you, that you have struck me these three times?'" (Numbers 22:28) During my childhood, it was imperative to believe in a talking donkey. In defense of this miraculous story, I can remember an older church member proclaiming, "If God says the donkey talked, then the donkey talked. There is nothing to argue about. It's a talking donkey. Just remember, son, God works in mysterious ways." Unfortunately, this limited view of the Bible excludes the opportunity to view Scripture as a beautiful allegory to explain our spiritual ancestors' understanding of God.

The majority of our church community believed science stood in opposition to God. More than once, I can remember a Sunday School teacher becoming visibly upset when the word evolution was mentioned. For our church community, it was essential to accept every word in the Bible as an indisputable

18   ANDY KONIGSMARK

fact. By gosh, if the Bible says God took a rib from Adam to create Eve, then that's exactly what happened.

Our pastor loved to warn the congregation about the forces of evil. The stronger we grew in faith, the more the devil would seek to destroy us. The devil was constantly lurking, searching for opportunities to destroy our faith in God. The Christian faithful must remain on alert. The world works day and night to pull us away from the arms of Jesus. Hollywood is controlled by the hands of the devil, which delivered extreme power to evil men trying to pollute our minds with filth. Rock bands encouraged young people to have sex, take drugs, and abandon their moral compass. *Dungeons and Dragons* was a gateway to witchcraft. The pastor's message was clear: Satan is capitalizing on worldly influences to destroy our lives.

It was taught that any non-Christian was going to burn in hell, and hell was described in lurid detail. This powerful imagery is scary for anyone to hear, not just children. I didn't even have a clear understanding of heaven or hell. I was unable to grasp the idea of Satan. But I had visions of people screaming, consumed in flames but eternally unable to die.

As a young child, I was terrified by my visions of hell. Sometimes I would have a hard time going to sleep at night. I was scared of a red man with pointy horns, a long tail, and a pitchfork waiting to pierce my flesh the moment I fell asleep. I thought any time I committed a sin or disobeyed God, my parents, or my church, I was going to hell. Every day, I was building up an unforgivable list of sins. If I wanted to go to heaven with my family, I was told, I had to cleanse myself of all that disgusting filth. To reach the heaven of Christians, I must beg God for forgiveness and believe Jesus Christ saved me from my sins. If I did not accept Jesus's salvation, I was going to be dragged into the depths of hell to suffer for all eternity.

In this fear-based theology, we choose heaven to avoid hell. Adults in my church allowed us to believe hell was filled with murderers, rapists, witches and warlocks. It was the must awful scenario an eight-year-old could imagine. Adults preyed upon church members' fears of hell. Thus, we were raised with an anti-hell theology. We would do anything to avoid hell, and this meant accepting Jesus Christ as our savior to earn our "fire insurance." We wouldn't have to go to hell. We wouldn't burn for eternity. We wouldn't live with the devil. We wouldn't be eternally separated from our family.

On Sunday mornings, the message was clear. We can freely choose to go to heaven or hell. It is our choice. No one is going to choose hell, which led to hundreds of people racing down the aisles on Sunday morning to ask the senior pastor to save them from it. As children, we were not seeking a personal relationship with Jesus Christ. We didn't read the Bible to grow closer to God. We ran toward Jesus because we were so afraid of going to hell.

I was always welcome at church until I began asking questions. At the age of ten, I was removed from Sunday School because I was becoming a bad influence on the other children. I became a pariah when I asked the unthinkable—"I heard Kareem Abdul Jabbar is a Muslim. Does this mean he's going to hell?" Case closed. Parents were called, friends were warned, and our family was reprimanded.

JUST AWFUL

As an eight-year-old, everyone within our Christian community tip-toed around the word sex. When evil thoughts of sexuality began creeping into our feeble brains, every adult in the congregation became quieter than a mouse peeing on cotton. As an elementary school student, I did not know much about sex, except a teenager's raging hormones were the work of the Devil. Within the evangelical purity movement, it was essential to save sex for marriage to be a good Christian.

I still cringe, recalling this memory. First Mega Church was filled to the brim this particular Sunday morning. Our church could comfortably seat 2,500 audience members. This does not include the overflow rooms or the millions of people watching at home. At the beginning of service, my brother's youth group friend, Brett, walked onto the stage. His hands were shaking as he picked up the microphone. His first few words were barely audible. Someone from the audience encouraged him to speak up.

With tears streaming down his face, Brett said, "I came on stage this morning to ask for forgiveness. I have sinned. Last week, we discovered my girlfriend was pregnant. We were having premarital sex, and she got pregnant. We knew it was wrong, but we kept sinning against God. I am so sorry. This morning, I'm trying to ask everyone for their forgiveness. I have already asked Alicia's parents for forgiveness. I have asked my parents for forgiveness. Now, I'm asking everyone in the congregation for forgiveness. I admit what we did was wrong. To make things right, Alicia and I and will be getting married next month. We will start a family and raise the baby together. If there are any high school students in here having sex, please stop. It's not worth it. Sex is meant to be saved for marriage. Please learn from my mistakes before it's too late."

The words were received by the congregation with deafening silence. We stared in complete disbelief as Brett became a lamb voluntarily walking into the slaughterhouse, knowing full well what his fate would be. In that shameful moment, thousands of church members witnessed his youthful spirit shrivel and die. With a shaky hand, he returned the microphone to the stand. The deacons hurried to the pulpit and ushered him offstage.

Some thirty years later, I can still painfully recall Brett enduring public scrutiny at the hands of his church. After he exited the stage, everything became a blur. Part of my innocence was also destroyed that morning just from watching him and feeling his shame.

When I turned twelve, the church youth group hit fast-forward on the world of sex. Youth leaders constantly reminded everyone that sex outside of marriage is a sin. Their theology— God created man and woman to enjoy sex only within the confines of marriage. The message: you are cheating on God, Jesus, and your future spouse if you have sex before you are married.

Until I hit puberty, I was not scared of sex, but I was terrified of sin. Through a narrow conservative viewpoint, I came to understand all forms of sin would lead to eternity in hell. To enter the gates of heaven, I must avoid sin. When I became a teenager, the sinfulness of premarital sex was a constant theme within youth group. We were well aware that a kiss from an attractive girl could cause us to lose our most sacred possession: our virginity. The guilt-riddled conclusion—sex before marriage is a gateway to hell.

Our youth leaders denounced all sexual thoughts as wicked, sinful practices. The Sports Illustrated Swimsuit Edition was to be avoided because it is a gateway to pornography—yet another path to hell. Scantily-clad women were trying to trick us into having sex. Furthermore, it is wrong, nasty, and disgraceful to touch oneself. We should only touch ourselves while taking a bath or shower. The youth pastor allowed us to believe that touching oneself in a sexual manner is a one of the most sala-cious forms of backsliding. Based on this logic, the act of masturbation is sending millions of teenage boys straight to hell. In response, young men must be shielded from all sexual imagery. We clung to the phrase "Flee, baby, flee" in regard to sexual temptation. If it feels good, it's wrong. If you do it in secret, it's wrong. If it feels wrong, then it's definitely wrong. If it's wrong, just know it's wrong. If she gets pregnant, you're most certainly going to hell.

CHAPTER 3

MIDDLE SCHOOL TORTURE

"I have never been jealous. Not even when my dad finished fifth grade a year before I did."—Jeff Foxworthy

WELCOME TO MISERY SCHOOL

If anyone tells you middle school was the best years of their life, feel sorry for them. There is nothing glamorous about these prepubescent years except dodgeball. Take away dodgeball, and you're left with *Lord of Flies* meets *Axe Body Spray*.

Sixth grade is an unfortunate time for everyone, especially for a special needs kid who barely stood four feet tall. Not only was I painfully short, but I was awkward in every way. My life was filled with bad haircuts, unfortunate hand-me-downs, and old sneakers.

One painful moment occurred when my mother offered to sew me a pair of homemade parachute pants—those gigantic, diaper-shaped pants made infamous by MC Hammer. Hot off the press, I pulled on my nightclub-inspired attire and rushed to the school bus filled with excitement. The moment I walked into school, a classmate yelled out, "I love that trash bag you're wearing." Another student asked, "Are those your grandad's pampers?" Even my teacher said, "Well! That's an interesting outfit, Andy." Without responding, I ran to the locker room and tossed my Hammer pants in the trash. For the rest of the day, I wore my dirty gym clothes. Damn, middle school kids are mean!

THESE ARE THE RULES

My mother had several rules when we were children. Most were easy to abide by. However, one of them almost ruined my life in middle school. Every six months, we were given forty dollars to buy a brand-new pair of shoes. If we wanted anything more expensive, we had to use our own money. Throughout elementary school, I never thought about my shoes. "Who cares about my clothes?" I thought. "Especially shoes!" (This was long before the Hammer pants fiasco.) But on my first day of middle school, almost every other boy was wearing brand new Nikes. I quickly noticed that one's popularity was intricately connected to the coolness level of his shoes. I was wearing worn-out beach shoes. They had served their purpose—protecting my feet—but they were the equivalent of driving a dirty, twenty-year-old minivan when everyone else was rolling in brand new luxury cars. Oh, the horror!

When I arrived home, I begged my mom to buy me a new pair of high tops so I could fit in with the other kids. She thought about it for a moment and listened to my passionate argument. After dinner, she drove to Payless Shoes and we picked up a pair of all-white Jordache High Tops. I couldn't believe it—with one simple purchase, I had entered a whole new world of cool. I ran around our house all night in those shoes. I swore they instantly made me run faster, jump higher, and lift more weight. They were so cool, I even slept in them. The next day, I ran into my homeroom, excited to show off my shoes. I knew everyone would be sweating the new ride on my feet. I had just traded in my clunker for a brand-new Mercedes with all the extras. White Jordache High Tops with red highlights. Does it get any cooler?

The answer is yes. Immediately, all the kids started making fun of my shoes because they weren't Nikes or Reeboks. I remember the kids making comments like:

"I guess you bought Air Jordache because you couldn't afford Air Jordans."

"Are those shoes autographed . . . by the manager at K-Mart?"

"Here's a marker if you want to draw your own Swoosh."

I ran to the bathroom and cried. I stuffed my Jordache High Tops into my backpack and walked around the rest of the day in my socks. That night, I threw them in my closet and never wore them again. For the next three years of middle school, I saved every dime to buy the newest pair of Nikes. My whole world revolved around tennis shoes. I didn't care about anything else. My value as a human being was equivalent to the value of my shoes.

CHAPTER 4

NO SO HIGH SCHOOL

"Never go to your high school reunion pregnant or they will think that is all you have done since you graduated."—Erma Bombeck

JIMMY TUCK

I don't know if you know much about the opossum, but they look like a rat hopped up on steroids that's been hitting the gym. They're stout venomous creatures with giant teeth and a nasty, long tail. These wild vermin are country strong. And one of the biggest differences between a rat and a possum is that possums are strictly nocturnal and live in trees.

Where I grew up, these nasty little suckers are all too common. They're not just mean-looking, they're actually mean. From time to time, I would see one of them dead on the side of the road. Most of the time, I wouldn't think anything about it, except for one day when I was driving in my truck, which was a low rider, with my friend, Deon. I ran over a possum, and the truck got stuck. That's right. The possum stopped the truck.

Deon and I pulled it out and threw it into the bushes by the side of the road. Then inspiration struck. Why waste it, we thought, when we can stick it on his girlfriend Autumn's front door instead? What a great idea, we thought. How hilarious it would be when they came home and saw a nasty, smelly, blood-drenched possum. That would really freak them out. What could possibly go wrong? Answer: Much.

We saw Autumn the next day at school and didn't want to bait her too much because she would figure out we were responsible.

"Anything weird happen yesterday?" I asked nonchalantly.

"That's funny you say that," she replied. "Our dog Lucky dragged a dead possum into the house."

This plan was going better than I ever could have anticipated.

"And he dragged that possum all over the house and got blood on the couch and the stairs. And then he dragged that dead possum up onto my parent's bed, then sat there and ate it on their bed. There was blood everywhere. Ruined their sheets, stained the couch, and got blood all over the stairs."

"That's awful," I said with genuine concern, while calculating the cost to repair all that damage.

Then she said, "Do you think somebody put that possum on my doorstep?"

I looked at her and said, "No, I don't know anybody mean enough to do something like that."

That should have scared us off from ever doing anything like that again, but it didn't. A couple of days later, Deon and I found a dead squirrel. I'm not sure what it died of because there was no blood on it. It was like it had died of shock. We just found it hanging out on the road as if it were having a nap. So, naturally, we did what anybody else would do after finding a dead squirrel —we picked it up, put it in my truck and started trying to figure out how to scare someone with it. The possum for Autumn turned out much better than we expected, so this time we decided to put the dead squirrel in Jimmy Tuck's mailbox. We envisioned old Jimbo going out to get the mail, seeing the squirrel and freaking out. In our minds, again, it was a brilliant idea.

I saw Jimmy the next day at school and casually asked, "Jimbo, what's really going on?"

"Not much, man," he said.

"How was the mail yesterday?" I said.

"I knew it!" he snapped. "I knew it was you! My mom went out to get the mail and fainted when she saw that squirrel!"

On the outside, I looked very concerned, but inside I was thinking this was better than expected yet again.

"I can't believe you did that! I'm going to get you back."

"Oh, come on. Take it easy. She just fainted."

"My mom could have died."

"Okay, number one, she couldn't have *died*. And number two, because she only fainted, it's a great practical joke."

He swore up and down that he was going to get me good, and he was as good as his word. I went out to my truck one morning a few days later, and there was a huge cat asleep on my truck. At least I thought it was a cat, and I thought it was asleep. I picked up a stick, walked slowly over to it, and poked it a few times.

"Get outta there! Get off my truck!"

It didn't move. That's when I realized it wasn't a cat—it was a big, dead, nasty raccoon. And it wasn't asleep, it was dead. I scraped it off, laid it in the back yard, and drove to school. The first thing I did was find Jimbo Tuck and demanded to know if he put the raccoon on my car.

"I don't know what you're talking about," he said.

"Jimbo, you better fess up. You better fess up right now or it's going to get worse."

"I really don't know what you're talking about," he repeated.

"Jimbo, this is your last chance. Fess up!"

But Jimmy didn't fess up, so a feud started festering that was as bad as that dead raccoon.

Poor Jimmy was on my soccer team. An opportunity for revenge came one day when I may or may not have hidden his soccer cleats and uniform minutes before the first game of the season. I may or may not have played a lot of mean tricks on Jimmy that year, and every time he confronted me, I said, "As soon as you admit to dumping that raccoon on my car, I'll leave you alone."

My dad always stirred the pot when he saw Jimmy. He'd say, "Jimbo, why don't you just admit that you put that raccoon on Andy's car?"

And I'd add, "Yeah, Jimbo, just admit it."

I tortured poor Jimmy. My entire senior year, I tortured that poor kid, saying over and over, "Just admit it—just admit you put that raccoon on my car, Jimmy."

I graduated college a few years later, and my dad said to me, "Andy, remember that time I put that raccoon on your car and you blamed Jimmy Tuck?"

Have you heard or can you imagine the sound a descending elevator makes when the power shuts off? That's what I felt, complete with the stomach-turning feeling and suddenly pale complexion.

"Huh-wha-?" I said.

"It was me. Can't believe you never figured it out, especially after Jimmy never broke down and confessed. There was nothing to confess to!"

"That's something you could have told me at the time! I harassed poor Jimmy Tuck for an entire year until I went to college."

"Oh, yeah, guess I forgot to tell you," he said with a nonchalance that reminded me of me when I was asked about a certain other raccoon.

My only defense is things are handed down, such as total

lack of remorse for practical jokes. My own father was the one who put the raccoon on my car, but he let me attack poor old, innocent Jimmy. In the words of Freddie Mercury, Jimbo did his sentence but committed no crime.

DAILY MEDICATION

My freshman year of high school, there were 500 students in our class. At the time, it was the largest incoming class. Four years later, 250 of my fellow classmates had withdrawn from school for multiple reasons. At the time of my graduation, our high school was topping the charts in teen pregnancies, drug arrests, and dropout rate. Several friends and acquaintances were serving 5-10-year prison sentences before reaching their nineteenth birthdays.

During the first quarter, our school posted every student's grades outside the lunchroom. My grade point average was the second lowest in the entire ninth grade. Only Brian had lower grades, and that was because he dropped out of school to attend drug rehab. Upon receiving my pitiful grades, I was removed from the regular classroom. My new classes included Pre-Algebra, Basics of English, and Life Skills.

During this same time period, the first signs of mental illness began cropping up. Something was wrong, and no one could place their finger on the problem. Initially, my parents believed their impending divorce was creating the distress. The school counselor had other ideas. She believed my personal problems began surfacing when my older siblings left home. Friends and family members were convinced I was acting like a normal teenager. Despite the variety of opinions, summoning enough energy to face the day was becoming a laborious chore. No matter the root cause of my spiraling depression, I needed help.

Daily medication and weekly therapy were prescribed to provide balance and perspective. As expected, these mental challenges created additional problems in the classroom. This was not common knowledge at the time, but many students who struggle with dyslexia also deal with severe bouts of depression.

On a monthly basis, the teachers called home to discuss my excessive absences and general lack of enthusiasm. The principal called on multiple occasions to discuss my erratic, attention-seeking behavior. After the second call from the principal, I placed a call block on the local school system. Imagine my parents' surprise on conference day when they learned multiple phone calls had not been received.

Church attendance remained constant as emotional, social and family turmoil began swirling out of control. My Christian faith served as my moral compass; that is, until our Southern Baptist youth leader said I was a bad influence on the other kids. My gold hoop earrings, baggy clothes, and affinity for rap music set a bad tone for the other youth. His concerns led to my expulsion from Sunday School and certain youth activities. Church should have been a safe place, but now I was only welcome if I played by the rules.

SECRETS

By the time I reached my junior year of high school, life had become a never-ending game of Jenga. If one block became unstable, everything might come tumbling down. High school can be a tumultuous experience for kids of every creed and color. All a teenager needs to spice up the adventure is one-part bipolar condition mixed with two-parts conservative Christian values. The fire really begins to cook when you stir these key ingredients with school work, peer groups, and a part-time job at the local gas station.

In these years, busy-ness became my best friend. A full schedule hid the majority of depression, anxiety, and manic moments from the outside world. The road to emotional freedom was around the corner if I could maintain an intricate façade of happiness. This intricate balancing act hid my emotional pain that was trapped just beneath the surface. The bubble of busyness provided a shield of protection; until my parent's marriage reached the breaking point. For years, their relationship reflected the exquisite beauty of a Norman Rockwell painting. Our local Christian community placed their marriage upon a fabricated pedestal.

For the sake of their children, our parents kept their struggles hidden from the world. Their impending divorce would spark a juicy supply of gossip at the local hair salon; but there was no scandal, physical abuse or extra-marital affair. Their marriage was broken. Lines of communication were shut down. The desire to fight for the relationship had left the building. And when my parents could no longer hide their pain and loneliness, they made the painful decision to end the marriage.

Playing the role of disconnected teenager, I was oblivious to the problems facing my mom and dad. Needless to say, their decision to separate came as a total surprise. Friends, family, and neighbors were shocked to hear about their divorce. This must be a joke; my parents were not getting a divorce. Sure, other kids' parents might get a divorce but not my parents. Despite loads of denial from all parties involved, their marriage was over.

SPIRALING

With life spiraling out of control, a concerned high school guidance counselor arranged a family intervention. As the meeting began, the counselor bluntly stated, "Well, it's not like he is going to Duke or anything. To be honest, Mrs. Konigsmark, Andy will be lucky to graduate high school. He should consider joining a branch of the military. Or maybe we can find a good trade to learn. The truth is, not every student is destined for college."

Based on test scores and classroom performance, her words held merit. The message could have been delivered more tactfully, but her observations were correct. Attending college had never been my dream. I didn't enjoy receiving a new syllabus and reading log for the semester. I dreaded thirty-minute lectures. From the day I entered kindergarten, academics had never been my sweet spot. As a result, I saw no reason to chase higher education after high school. I had plans to buy a new Ford Mustang, live on some land in the country, and pay my bills as an auto-mechanic.

Yet, the guidance counselor's lackluster intervention created a ripple effect. As my mother and I walked out of the office, a passion for something greater began to build. This conversation marked a major turning point in life. I wouldn't let an outsider's ill-conceived words define my story. An incredible adventure was waiting beyond the Georgia state line. I just needed the proper fuel to propel the journey. Over the next several weeks and months, I gathered the resolve to experience everything our world has to offer. I wouldn't settle for the status quo. With a bit of luck and immense support from my family, I would create a better narrative than I could have ever imagined.

CHAPTER 5

BI-POLAR BEAR

"Part of my act is meant to shake you up. It looks like I'm being funny, but I'm reminding you of other things. Life is tough, darling. Life is hard. And we better laugh at everything; otherwise, we're going down the tube."—Joan Rivers

THE NOOGIE

What is your initial response when you act out of character? Most people silently ask themselves, "What was I thinking?" In high school, one of these moments occurred when I grabbed my Spanish teacher to deliver not homework or some overdue assignment, but a noogie. In case you are unfamiliar with the term, a noogie occurs when a knuckle—usually the middle one—is forcefully rubbed back and forth on an innocent bystander's head. This action often causes hair displacement and mild cursing. Much to everyone's surprise, this malicious attack took place in the middle of the busy lunchroom. During this single-knuckle assault, with great enthusiasm, I yelled, "Noogie!" I was out of control and needed to announce the juvenile crime to the entire world. It was a terrible idea that led to large amounts of hair dishevelment.

The little devil sitting on my shoulder was encouraging the decision. The other angel must have gone to the restroom because he was nowhere to be found. Maybe he jumped ship in horror the moment he saw me eyeing her scalp and baring my knuckle. Without question, my actions were inexcusable, and I deserved to be punished.

I can't imagine what this poor teacher told her boyfriend later that night—"I was at the salad bar minding my own business, and all of a sudden, this kid grabbed me and started grinding his knuckle into my cranium."

It was only natural when the teacher flipped out. I had failed Spanish the previous semester, so I was thankful that her tirade was at least in English. Her outburst of emotions consisted of anger, total shock, anger, humiliation, outrage, and more anger.

The next day, I was informed by our principal that the teacher was planning to file sexual harassment charges. Charging a high school student with sexual harassment was pretty harsh considering I was still a virgin and there's nothing sexual about a noogie. Mercifully, the teacher dropped the charges after a local psychologist diagnosed me with a bipolar disorder. A month of Saturday morning detention became the punishment—a pretty light sentence considering the fact that noogies are usually delivered by larger children to smaller ones. In fact, it may have been the only time in human history a student has given one to a teacher, and for no reason but fun, no less.

Take-away: authority figures don't like to be treated like little brother/sisters in front of the entire student body.

IT WAS REAL DARK

I was fourteen when I first began experiencing a deep, dark depression. After school, I would take the stairs down to the basement and crawl in bed until dinnertime. With enough prompting, I would struggle free from my self-constructed cocoon. Dragging myself into the kitchen for dinner became a minor victory. Much to everyone's shock, a previously happy child was concealing large amounts of loneliness and despair. After dinner and a few minutes of homework, I would go back to sleep to avoid suicidal thoughts.

Unlike most teenagers, I despised the weekend. I spent Saturdays and Sundays hiding in my darkened bedroom instead of searching for romance or hanging out with friends. If anyone asked what was bothering me, I gave stock responses like "nothing's wrong" or "teenagers just need extra sleep" or "please stop asking what's wrong because everything is fine."

A few weeks before turning fifteen, I told my parents I didn't want to live anymore. Once the initial shock had passed, this devastating news was embraced with a deep sense of love and compassion, thank God. Part of the family backstory includes a paternal grandfather who was diagnosed with bipolar disorder. However, in his case, that diagnosis could not prevent his eventual suicide. As a little boy, my grandfather's death was kept secret from us and attributed to natural causes because of the shame connected with suicide.

My father was in his early twenties when his dad took his own life, and the event permanently changed his outlook on life. It must have been incredibly difficult for him to make sense of his dad's premature death. It's not an uncommon story, but it is always heartbreaking nonetheless. So, it must have been extra hard on my father when he heard his youngest son cry out, "I don't want to live anymore." Instead of ignoring a desperate cry for help, my parents sprang into action. They asked, "What can we do to save our son?"

I began to meet with a psychologist on a regular basis. Over the next couple of months, we experimented with a variety of antidepressants to regulate my emotional roller coaster. During this assessment period, I was diagnosed with bipolar disorder; more specifically, deep bouts of depression coupled with full-blown manic episodes. An individual suffering from a manic disorder has great difficulty controlling their actions. An "unattended bonfire" is a metaphor often used to explain manic episodes. Without proper care and attention, the bonfire will destroy everything in sight. The fire does not have feelings. It is only searching for fuel to continue burning. It will continue burning with intensity until something from the outside world contains it. However, even when controlled, the bonfire can continue raging without hurting anyone.

The bonfire metaphor is accurate for manic episodes, but it does not properly explain both sides of a bipolar disorder. The roller coaster metaphor more accurately explains the intricacies of the condition. As the ride begins traveling uphill, the mania rises. At the top of the roller coaster, the mania creates feelings of invincibility and pure ecstasy before plunging down to the bottom of the ride where crippling depression destroy all traces of the ecstasy felt only moments earlier. The bottom is a hopeless mess. But just like a roller coaster, an individual with a bipolar disorder does not stay at the bottom of the ride. The ride takes us back up the track to the euphoric, mania-induced high, and again we are on top of world. We are invincible. Then we sink down the track into the pits of despair again. If this vicious cycle is left untreated, the highs become higher and the lows become lower. At some point, the extreme nature of the disease controls the person's life. Thankfully, antidepressants are designed to decrease the extreme highs and lows. As a result, medicated individuals are able to avoid debilitating depressive episodes and gain control over manic outbursts.

In the midst of a manic episode, I was the life of the party. Friends and outsiders were drawn to the unmedicated whirling dervish. Peers witnessed the manic outbursts, but they could not understand the debilitating depression threatening to destroy my life. Close friends said unmedicated Andy was the best version. Yet they were absent while I was struggling to find reasons to get out of bed. Despite the depression, I promised anyone concerned about me that I would not kill myself. For much of high school and college, staying alive for my family became my only resolve. I did not want another suicide to cause our family unwanted pain or suffering. I was not chasing life to experience tomorrow. I was choosing to live to prevent others from experiencing sadness.

The story and diagnosis sound bleak, but the diagnosis of clinical depression provided life with an exciting spark to live. When a dark cloud of desperation seeks to grab hold, I jump on my mountain bike or grind out a ten-mile run. In Buddhist tradition, this is known as moving meditation. The euphoric endorphins slowly release and begin to cleanse the soul. I cherish these peaceful moments of exercise and use them to process life.

Even when I cannot exercise, I refuse to allow bipolar disorder to determine the outcome of my life. I embrace the world, searching for reasons to laugh. I will not let clinical depression steal my happiness. Through God's invincible strength, I direct my life toward joy. And as I chase adventure, depression fades in the rearview mirror. A mental illness will not destroy my life. Thanks to anti-depressants, exercise, and faith in God, I have found reasons to live.

Readers of Psalm 118:24 are reminded, "This is the day that the Lord has made; let us rejoice and be glad in it." Tomorrow is a new day, with exciting opportunities and a chance for a fresh start. To become victorious, we must place yesterday's trials and troubles aside. We have the power to write a new story. To embrace a different outcome, it is essential to search for joy and create space for uncontrollable laughter. Make it your mission to bring laughter and joy to others. When you are ready, embrace Divine guidance. Live each day as an occasion to bless everyone you meet. Look to the future and stop dwelling on yesterday's problems and traumas.

A PROGRESSIVE RESPONSE TO THE DEVIL

After the initial bipolar diagnosis, people in our conservative Christian community began blaming the devil for my problems. "There is nothing wrong with your mind; it's just the devil trying to destroy your life." Church members confronted my mother after church with, "Your son doesn't need antidepressants, he just needs God." These same people were willing to eat food loaded with preservatives but resisted modern medicine designed to regulate serotonin levels. When our son fell and needed stitches, no one from church told us to pray for a miraculous healing. He was rushed to the emergency room, and we offered prayers of gratitude for the doctors. Churches must remind congregations that modern medicine is not the enemy. Wellbutrin is not trying to replace the authority of God, yet these small-minded beliefs about science and medicine are pushing future generations of Americans further away from God's grace.

In Georgia, it was common practice to blame the devil for our problems. Instead of examining our own shortcomings, people loved to claim, "the devil made me do it." This simple catchphrase has affected the way many people understand the presence of evil. We believe the devil has the power to make us do things. But as my grandmother used to say, "The devil ain't going to waste his time messing with little old Andy Konigsmark." However, many people think they are important enough for the devil to take a personal interest in them, so they continue to envision a pitchfork-wielding creature whispering evil thoughts into their ears while the chubby little angel perched on their other shoulder tries to thwart the temptations of the devil. As someone who struggles with mental illness, I am certain the juxtaposition of good versus evil does not cause bipolar disorders.

For thousands of years, the world has been rejecting accountability. Instead of addressing our personal path of self-destruction, we shift blame to an external force of evil. From the beginning of time, humans have been pointing the finger at other people. In the creation story found in Genesis, the first humans are found passing blame. After eating forbidden fruit from the tree of knowledge, Adam and Eve are confronted by God. Instead of accepting responsibility for his actions, Adam blames Eve. "She gave me some fruit from the tree, and I ate it." After listening to the indictment from her lover, Eve also refuses to accept responsibility for her actions. Now, she must find someone or something to blame. Ultimately, she points the finger at the serpent. This story teaches the destructive power of blame. To create space for personal growth, we must start accepting responsibility for our actions.

I was a sophomore in college when the world learned Princess Diana had died in an automobile crash. Shortly after the tragic event, well-known Christian author Phillip Yancy began to receive numerous phone calls to appear on radio and television shows. These interviews usually started with some form of the demand, "We want you to explain how God could possibly allow such a terrible accident." On one of these shows, without thinking, Yancy tersely replied, "Could it have had something to do with a drunk driver going ninety miles an hour in a narrow tunnel? How exactly was God involved?" Instead of pointing fingers at God, we must examine how the children of God can bring healing into this broken world.

Despite personal resistance, fellow Christians continued to offer insensitive advice after discovering my mental health struggles, such as, "Andy, if you pray harder, God will take away your depression." This advice only creates tension in personal relationships. During my late teens and early twenties, I faithfully prayed for God to cure my bipolar disorder. Criticize all you want, but I am done with these prayers. Praying in this manner reduces God to a vending machine. I would rather offer prayers for the millions of children trapped in deplorable living conditions. It is difficult to focus on petty problems when innocent children do not have proper access to clean water and food.

To move forward, we must stop attacking the faith of others. We must find ways to connect. Critiquing someone's prayer life is not a recipe for success. Instead of using prayer to change God, we must allow prayer to change us. Prayer becomes transformational when we are open to the practice and to the connection with the Divine. However, it becomes watered down when we start asking God for parking spaces at the shopping mall. With much gratitude, the majority of my teenage prayers were not answered. For two straight years, I prayed for a V-8 Mustang GT:

"Dear Lord, all I want is a sweet muscle car, a mullet, and maybe nice toenails. But I'll settle for the rumble of eight cylinders. Amen."

God did not answer this amazing prayer, but it does not mean prayer is not powerful. I would have settled for a Jeep Wrangler with a six-inch lift and 38-inch tires; I could grow the mullet on my own time. If I really wanted a Mustang, I should have worked harder and saved more money. Yet the desire for this car was a selfish endeavor. In hindsight, I should have redirected all of my time, energy, and finances toward serving others living on the margins of society: the same people Jesus desperately loves. More powerful than a brand-new sports car is developing the path for children to break the cycle of poverty.

CHAPTER 6

LOOK, MA! I MADE IT!

"College is the reward for surviving high school."—Judd Apatow

COLLEGE

For many, college is not a destination but a transformational journey. During these life-changing years, we transition from childhood into adulthood. The moment our parents drive away, we begin embracing a newfound freedom. For the first time, no one is looking over our shoulders constantly. As we step onto campus, our new friends invite us to a keg party. They promise loud music, beer, and maybe a little marijuana. The next morning, our heads are throbbing as we oversleep for our first class. Despite the ringing between our ears, the picture of freedom begins to form. We have earned the right to skip class. No one is telling us we drank too much last night. We are finally free to make our own mistakes.

During college, new challenges present themselves for those raised in a conservative Christian home. On Sunday mornings, no one is pressuring or encouraging us to attend church. The guilt and shame of missing worship service slowly begins to evaporate. No one is holding our hands, and success and failure become our sole responsibility. Most graduating seniors view college with a sense of wonder and excitement. I did not fall into this category. Two years before graduation, I began working at a local automotive shop. Making money, working hard, and learning about cars became an addiction. Learning to become a mechanic became the priority. Upon graduating high school, I planned to work seventy hours a week at the local Ford dealership, purchase a muscled-up Mustang, and get married, all within five years.

Everything was going according to plan until my father pulled me aside and said, "Son, you have the rest of your life to work on cars. I can understand the desire to work with your hands. It's a rewarding profession filled with hard work. But hear me out on this. Your opportunity to attend college is now. Just try it for a year. If you don't enjoy the experience, you have my full support to return to the service station. College is not going to cost you a dime. The day you were born, your mother and I began saving for your college education."

College became a distant vision the longer I worked for the shop. I enjoyed the paycheck, the hard work, and comradery with my coworkers. These people became my second family; even the guy whose shirt was embroidered "Tarl." We affectionately called him Carl with a "T." Around three o'clock, we would pick up the intercom and start barking, "Carl with a T, your mom is on line one. She wants to know if you have enough clean underwear for the week. Sorry, Tarlton, you have another call on line two. It's your girlfriend. She needs you to pick her up after cheer practice."

Much to my surprise, a number of Americans have the first name Tarl. Many of these unfortunate souls are named after Tarl Cabot, the principal character in a science fiction series by John Norman titled *Tarnsman of Gor*.

One of my other coworkers was Flying Brian. He earned his

name by telling tall tales about beating up Chuck Norris with a spinning roundhouse kick. Another coworker, Stacy, earned the unfortunate nickname of Fat Back at the age of six because of a drunk uncle.

Heeding my father's sound advice, I bid adieu to my coworkers Tarl, Flying Brian, and Fat Back. A week later, I registered for classes at Belhaven College in Jackson, Mississippi. Based on my high school performance and college placement test, I registered for Basic Math, Remedial English, and Art. Not the traditional approach to academic success.

After our first English test, my professor asked me to meet her in her office after class. "Andy, you received the absolute worst score in the class. I cannot believe your high school would allow you to graduate. Without question, you need extra tutoring."

Until this point, no one critically scrutinized my poor grammar or lack of writing development. She concluded the conversation by adding, "To pass my class, you must attend hour-long tutoring sessions in my office after every class."

After my second failed assignment, the professor called me into her office again. "Andy, you are making improvements, but you still have a lot of hard work ahead of you. I will not fail you if we continue to work on your writing every day after class. I promise, your hard work will be rewarded."

For the next eight weeks, I faithfully attended tutoring sessions with my professor. Fully invested in the process, I focused on improving my writing during nights and weekends. I paid dormmates to edit my papers. Much to my embarrassment, I was given extra homework, vocabulary lists, and grammar flash cards.

At the end of the semester, I was shocked when I received my report card. My grade for Remedial English was a Big Fat F. Armed with a trusty glue gun and Bedazzler kit, I received an A plus for Art class. Basic Math presented hordes of difficult equations and problems, but I still managed a solid C. For all non-math wizards, these combined letters equal a pitiful first semester.

After receiving my report card, I went straight to my professor's office. "There must be some mistake because there's a Big Fat F on my report card. We had a deal. We agreed you wouldn't fail me if I came for tutoring every day."

Without hesitation she responded, "Yes, that's what we agreed to."

Incredulous, I asked, "Then why do I have an F?"

Offering little compassion, she justified her decision. "Andy, I just couldn't give you a passing grade. You did everything I asked, but your writing is atrocious. If I let you pass, I would be doing you an immense disservice. To maintain a clean conscious, I cannot give you a passing grade. However, you are welcome to retake my class next semester."

Instead of retaking the professor's English class, I went back to my sad dorm room and packed all five of my worldly possessions. Next, I marched over to the Dean's office to inform them of my decision to withdraw from classes. Instead of begging me to stay, they wished me a safe trip home. Twenty minutes later, I was driving back to Georgia with my tail tucked between my legs. Regrets and insecurities began to form as I cruised down the highway.

This would have been a great opportunity for my father to say, "Son, you should never rush a major decision." Instead, I was surprised when my parents welcomed me with open arms. There was no judgment or ridicule, only acceptance. Within days of moving home, I began taking classes at a local community college. With enough hard work, I would be able to transfer to the University of Georgia. If I was going to enjoy college, I needed to be a Georgia Bulldog.

I entered this fragile world with red and black running through my and my family's veins. Saturday mornings in the fall were spent listening to legendary announcer Larry Munson and the Georgia Red Coat Marching Band. Before I was born, my father received a full athletic scholarship to play football for his beloved Bulldogs. My mother, aunts, uncles, and brother were also graduates of the United States' oldest Public University, The University of Georgia, home of the Bulldogs.

Despite all of my academic shortcomings, my community college professor embraced my raw writing style. She was not fixated on structure or grammatical errors. Instead, she focused on reader connection and story development. Some of the advanced writing techniques were becoming hardwired.

At the end of the semester, the community college professor conceded, "You're not a great writer, but there's a rough elegance to your style." It was the equivalent of saying, "You might be really handsome if you got a nose job."

For the entirety of my college career, I produced a gluttonous supply of grammatically and structurally flawed papers. These assignments contained enough adverbs, haphazard punctuation marks, and run-on sentences to fill Sanford Stadium.

After spending three semesters raising my GPA, I transferred to the University of Georgia. From my prospective, I had reached the pinnacle of my academic career. My degree and future job prospects were of little concern. I was going to be a Georgia Bulldog, which signaled smooth sailing. "Ain't nothing finer in the land than a drunk, obnoxious Georgia fan."

On paper, the University of Georgia was everything I longed for, yet it never provided a sense of belonging or community. I struggled to find my social rhythm. Most weekends, I dealt with the insecurities of an uninvited house guest. Friends and classmates encouraged me to enjoy my college experience. From their point of view, I was missing out because I had zero interest in drinking or partying.

During my junior year at Georgia, one question changed the trajectory of my life. Out of the blue, one of my best friends asked, "Do you want to transfer to University of Montana? I've always had this dream of moving to the mountains and never coming home. Wanna join me?" I had never considered moving across the country, but I was not loving my experience at Georgia.

Six months later, we moved to Missoula, Montana. Within a few short weeks, we began a life-altering experience. I began working as a poker dealer, snowboarding became my new passion, and I began an affair with the outdoors. I understood Montana, and its people embraced me and my silly Southern accent. Our new friends were more concerned with creating epic adventures than partying on the weekends.

By the time I enrolled at Montana, I had already failed Latin and Spanish. Managing dyslexia and learning a foreign language was a grueling endeavor. As a special-needs student, I was given the option to learn statistics as my foreign language. You read that right. My foreign language is numbers because it's an international language. I am fluent in Japanese statistics, French equations, and Swahili algebra, but I can't speak a lick of Spanish.

The year before transferring, Montana added a writing exit exam for every graduating senior. A week before graduation, my roommate and I huddled in a small classroom to complete our writing assignment. For the next three hours, I poured sweat over my paper. The little voice inside my head kept saying, "You have to pass. You have to pass. Your family is coming to graduation. Andy, you have to pass this writing exam."

During writing breaks, I broke my own rule and called upon a vending machine version of God. "God, I'm ashamed to ask for help. I'm sorry for placing our relationship on the back-burner, but I really need your help. Please, Lord, please let me pass this writing exam. I promise to be faithful if you just help me pass. I will give you all the glory."

Despite my pleas for God's Divine intervention, I failed the writing exam. After five long years of hard work and sacrifice, I would not be allowed to walk with my classmates. This embarrassing failure created a wave of negative emotions. Debilitating anxiety consumed my thoughts, and clinical depression filled my head with lies.

The morning before graduation, I begged for another chance to pass the writing exam. "Please give me another chance, Dean Howard. My entire family is flying out to attend graduation. Please just give me one more chance to pass the exam."

A few hours later, Dean Howard granted permission to retake the exam. I began rubbing the magic lamp, summoning God's help the moment I walked into the classroom. "Heavenly Father, my family will be here this afternoon. I'm sure this is not a surprise to you because you are God. I am not asking for much. But, please, let me pass this writing exam. Please, God, I have worked so hard. Just help me find favor with the person reading my paper. Please, God."

When we pray in this manner, we are not listening to God. Instead, we are trying to force our will on God. Prayer becomes nothing more than a Christmas wish list. Without proper appreciation for prayer, we unwittingly place limits on the power, mercy, and grace of God. When practiced with an open heart, prayer changes us.

Prayer did not change the exam grade. I failed a second time. Intense feelings of failure and embarrassment began to form. Instead of focusing on the positive aspects of my life, I became angry with God for not listening to my prayers. I was consumed with negative self-talk and blamed the school for asking students to complete an exit exam. Engaging in periods of self-pity belittles the actual pain and suffering taking place in the world.

Graduation morning was filled with unbearable anxiety, stress and embarrassment. In less than an hour, I would meet my family for breakfast to deliver the bad news. There was not much to say or rehearse. I would meet my parents at the hotel and say, "Thanks for coming to celebrate, but I am not going to walk this afternoon. I failed the exit exam, and I will not be allowed to graduate until I pass. I'm really sorry you traveled all this way."

Moments before walking out the door, the phone started ringing. My gut reaction was to ignore the call until I noticed that it was coming from the university.

"Andy, this is Pamela in the registrar's office. We have been reviewing your file this morning, and the school has decided to waive your exit exam. This afternoon, you will graduate and walk with the rest of your class."

Pamela continued to offer a longer explanation for the school's decision, but I was too excited to listen to the details.

"Not to be rude, Pamela, but I don't care at this point. All that matters is crossing the finish line!" I was thankful beyond words that someone thought, "Give this young man his diploma and let him walk toward a beautiful Montana sunset."

CHAPTER 7

CLEAN COMICS AND DIRTY TOILETS

"A friend of mine has a trophy wife, but apparently, it wasn't first place."—Steven Wright

CROOKED TEETH

The year was 1998, and my precious girlfriend told me I would never explore the world beyond our state lines. To boost my confidence, she let everyone know I didn't possess the courage or skills to become a standup comic. For her final trick, she offered several suggestions I could use to hide my crooked teeth. She was right; it was time to stop wearing a camouflage retainer. To save face, it became imperative to stop strutting my unfortunate smile like a proud peacock. I now understand; my teeth resembled a crowd of New Yorker's squeezing into a subway car at rush hour.

Thankfully, my sweet father said, "Son, I reckon it's about time we get them teeth fixed."

If you are a parent reading this book, please do not wait until your child reaches college before offering to pay for braces. Just pile on more painful memories when your children are in middle school; let eighth grade be a birthday they want to forget. At twenty-one, no one should be asked if they can open a bottle of beer with their overbite. Life can be cruel. As parents, we are called to limit the damage.

A few years later, I left Georgia without the love of my life— sometimes I like to call her bone of my bone, flesh of my flesh. Thankfully, her slightly tipsy diatribe inspired me to begin a nationwide journey for a new life. I promised whoever would listen that I would never return to Georgia. I realize now that I developed a fear of being average. In the back of my mind, I incorrectly believed that moving back to my hometown meant I had failed in life.

I did not have a game plan for my life, but I knew something needed to change. To overcome, I needed to run forward rather than stumbling backward. Upon receiving the news that I was destined to be a crooked-toothed loser, I was wearing *Star Wars* T-shirts, living at home with my recently-divorced father, attending community college, and working at a local gas station.

Despite my inauspicious lifestyle and limited world view, I was about to take the comedy world by storm, or so I thought. I had been telling funny stories and entertaining people my whole life. I could no longer deny the world my immense comedic talents. With my gas station paycheck, I promptly enrolled in Jeff Justice's Stand-up Comedy class. After twelve weeks of writing, practicing, and performing, all fifteen partici- pants were invited to perform a five-minute stand-up set at Atlanta's very own Punchline Comedy Club.

The live performance signified a formal graduation from the comedy class. It was a particularly memorable moment as friends and family filled the audience to laugh and cheer for their favorite comedians. The entire evening was thoughtfully orchestrated to provide a safe introduction into the unforgiving world of standup comedy. For the majority of comedy school graduates, this live performance would stand as the pinnacle of their comedy career. I, on the other hand, had much greater ambitions. This initial performance would mark the beginning of an illustrious comedy career.

THE BIG NIGHT

The Sunday before The Punchline comedy show, I tore the anterior cruciate ligament in my left knee. This devastating sports injury is typically reserved for NFL running backs, professional skiers and Gold Medal gymnasts. In complete glory, I did it jumping off a chair to dunk a basketball. Yes, this freak injury occurred after my friend, mentor and former youth pastor, Chris Reny, predicted "someone is about to get hurt." As usual, he was right, and I was wrong. Nanoseconds after the words left his lips, I landed on the ground in a crumpled pile. Reverend Reny calmly walked over and said, "See, guys. It's all fun and games until someone gets their eye poked out."

Despite the painful injury, the show must go on. With crutches in tow, I hobbled onto the stage to begin my comedy career. Jeff Galloway, who served as the night's emcee, said, "The rest of the class couldn't stand this next performer, so we beat the crap out of him." I had no jokes about my crutches or my injury; I just acted like everything was normal. A comedic lesson I learned much later was to always mention the obvious. If you are wearing an eyepatch to cover your pink eye, you better open your set with "Ahoy, Maties!" or "Shiver me timbers!" For the love of all things holy, please do not act like wearing an eye patch or using crutches is the same as wearing socks.

With the proper introduction, I grabbed the mic, spit my gum into the audience and closed out the evening's show. My well-rehearsed routine of family-friendly jokes brought down the house. Typically, I am not one to gloat, but this performance signaled my formal entrance into the world of professional comedy. The ecstasy of conquering the spotlight reverberated within my soul. In that brief five-minutes in the spotlight, I had become a rocket ship prepared to launch into Christian comedy fame and fortune.

SWALLOW THE GUM AND WALK AWAY

Like an idiot, I walked onto the stage with a mouth full of Double-Mint gum. Here is an essential lesson in case you are unaware: never grab a microphone with a mouth full of gum. Matter of fact, it is only appropriate to chew gum in your home or during your professional baseball career. For most mortals, chewing gum is an unforgivable sin. If you find yourself in an awkward gum-chewing situation, swallow the gum. Do not, under any circumstance, spit the gum into an audience member's Mountain Dew or a bridesmaid's bouquet.

I painfully remember the tongue-lashing I received from the owner of the Punchline Comedy Club after I spit my gum into the audience.

"You're lucky I didn't come pull your scrawny ass offstage."

In hindsight, I should have swallowed the Hubba Bubba and patiently waited seven years for my stomach to digest the gum, or at least stuck it in my back pocket. Instead, I exited stage right into the insidious wrath of the club owner, who happened to be a decorated Vietnam veteran. As I recall, General Grouchy descended like a fighter pilot from the rafters. With the perfect amount of surprise, he soared through the air to annihilate my personal bubble. Before I could scream for help, his hands became a boa constrictor around my neck. With venom spewing from his pores, he shared his supreme commitment to patriotism. "You son of a bitch. I fought overseas to save your life. And now you repay my decorated military service with complete disrespect. Your ass wouldn't last fifteen minutes in the military."

Dang, this veteran was strong. His hands locked into place, and his glassy eyes drifted to a distant galaxy. The plan had gone bad. Thank goodness a security guard witnessed the attack and came to the rescue. As I broke free from the vice-like death grip, I fell to the ground gasping for air. With the first breath, I repeated the mantra: swallow the gum. Just swallow the gum and walk away.

DELUSIONAL

In my delusional mindset, I was ready for the lights, camera, and action of Hollywood. There was only one little problem—I was not good. My jokes were lame. My delivery was corny. My stage presence was terrible. Sure, I understood the basic premise of a joke—setup/punchline—but at the end of the day, I was just a guy with enough courage to stand in front of an audience armed with a microphone and a cacophony of useless stories with weak payoffs. Telling jokes and being a stand-up comic are two different things. Anybody can tell a joke—but being a comedian is an art.

Something most people don't consider is that for many comedians, the stage serves as an office for a therapy session. We come onto the stage guided by our deepest fears, insecurities, and shortcomings. To heal, we poke holes in the fragile windows of our life. We find humor in the recesses of depression, alcoholism, and heartbreak. When we openly address the pain with humor, we move through the process and begin to steal power from some of our darkest moments.

For the past twenty years, I have walked onstage to face some of the most tragic moments of my life, often reluctantly, sort of like barely escaping from a haunted house but needing to go back inside to retrieve something important I can't live without.

For instance, when I was sixteen years old, my high school girlfriend became pregnant by someone else. I loved her response to the situation: "I'm not sure how this happened; I just got pregnant." She casually dismissed her pregnancy as if it were a common cold. Naturally, I responded with immense grace and compassion. "Of course, I love you, but just so you know—you *got* problems, you *got* milk, but you don't just *got* pregnant."

WE ARE IN CONTROL

No one deserves the labels emotionally unstable, insecure, or out of control. Yet, we assign these negative labels to our world on a daily basis. Somewhere deep within our biological framework, we've developed an innate desire to assign labels. These labels create a system to place people into categories. An example from high school might be jocks, nerds, or burnouts. As people land in particular categories, it is difficult to change the world's perceptions.

As a result, it is common practice to hide many of the personal issues we encounter. We hide our problems to distance ourselves from a negative stigma. Our egos struggle to thrive when we become trapped in undesirable categories. No one seeks the title of crazy person who lives next door. Ultimately, we are desperate to be known for our character, not by the issues we hide.

In response to the categories the world loves to form, I've invited audiences to laugh about my litany of issues and challenges. Thankfully, I was only diagnosed with dyslexia, attention deficit disorder, and mild stupidity. As we have been reminded by many, you can't fix stupid, but you sure can laugh about it.

I see these perceived issues as perfect joke material. A willingness to embrace self-deprecating humor robs mental illness of its power. By addressing perceived problems, I prevent people from earning an advanced degree in amateur psychology. Five minutes and a microphone are all I need to tear apart the host of learning disabilities I've encountered. The point—the audience connects with self-deprecating humor. As a result, when we control the flow of information, we remain in control of our life story.

BOMBING

Bombing on stage is one of the greatest fears people have about attempting to perform stand-up comedy, yet it is essential to fail on stage. In failure, growth occurs. We can never rise to the top if we never give ourselves a chance to sink to the bottom.

In the first year of trying to become America's next great comic, I made a complete fool of myself at Chris Tucker's Comedy Club in Atlanta. At this point in time, Chris Tucker was near the height of his Hollywood fame. He was a well-known comedian and earned big screen recognition with co-star Jackie Chan in *Rush Hour.*

In case you haven't figured this out by now, I am a skinny white kid with a heavy southern accent. One of my best friends from childhood is black, but this does not mean I understand black culture. My longtime high school girlfriend was black, but her older sister called me White Devil. Her father was a really big fan of mine, though. One time he even spoke to me. He said, "Don't eat my food." It was not the olive branch I was expecting, but I am certain somewhere in the deep recesses of his heart, he would have discovered the generosity to share a couple of stale chips. In short, my Anglo-Saxon DNA and white-collar childhood did not guarantee success at a predominantly black comedy club.

I arrived at Tucker's club three hours early to sign up for my first open mic. I brought my new girlfriend to the show, planning to impress her with my chops on the microphone. I envisioned walking onto the stage and winning the audience over. They were going to love me and my material. There's a lot to be said for positive visualization, but in hindsight, this was pure stupidity on my part.

Again, having the courage to get on stage and regurgitate some jokes didn't make me a comic. Nope, I was just some lame white kid in oversized jeans reciting jokes into a microphone. There was no passion in my comedy. No personal connection with the audience. I did not understand the rhythm and cadence to delivering a comedy set. I knew to pause for laughter, but that's only necessary if the audience laughs. It never crossed my mind that the audience would not connect with my unbelievable college roommate jokes.

With as much confidence as I could muster, I crossed the stage as the emcee announced, "Let's welcome to the stage our first comic, with a last name I can't pronounce . . . Andy!" I confidently grabbed the mic and launched into my first joke.

"So, my college roommate has a lot in common with her pet rabbit. They skip class, hop onto the couch naked, and they literally leave their crap everywhere."

All I heard from the audience was crickets after the punchline. My girlfriend didn't even laugh. Instead, I watched her sneak out the side door to avoid further humiliation. As I started to deliver my second joke, the DJ starting scratching on the turntables. The emcee hustled to the stage and grabbed the mic, "Yo, yo! Andy, that joke was whack!"

The good news is he was only able to mildly humiliate me one more time before I left the stage.

"Sorry about that last comic, and please forgive us, but the next comic is also white."

The emcee took a moment to collect his thoughts and then

looked at the audience. "Damn, I thought this was supposed to be a black comedy club."

As I was running out the back door of the club to avoid further shame, the other white comic grabbed the mic to make one more comment, "Yo, son, why don't you come back with some real jokes after you hit puberty."

Here is the truth—all comedians bomb on stage. It is just a price you pay to play the game, but I didn't know that at the time. I wish another comedian could have patted me on the back and said, "Don't worry, you'll knock 'em dead next time." Instead, I drove my girlfriend home, and we sat in total silence. I was secretly hoping she would try to make a quick getaway as we raced down the highway. Instead, we just sat there and wallowed in my deflated ego.

The good news is she waited several months before stabbing me in the back. I don't mean metaphorically. She literally plunged a knife into my back while we were doing the dishes, and on my twenty-first birthday, no less. I jumped, screamed and yelled the moment I felt the knife penetrate my skin. Naturally, with shock and horror, I asked, "Did you just stab me?"

She looked at me indignantly for a few seconds, then replied, "I did not stab you."

I was incredulous. "You are holding a knife dripping with blood, and I am bleeding. There's nobody else in the room. Please tell me who stabbed me if it wasn't you."

I swear, this was her explanation: "You upset me, so I was making a stabbing motion behind your back, and you backed into the knife. Basically, it's your fault for running into the knife."

The knife-wielding love interest is great for a movie script. However, in real life, it does not set a healthy precedent for a meaningful romantic relationship. Recovering from a knife wound is not the best way to celebrate love on one's birthday. In my delusional mind, though, this aspiring murderer was destined to become the future Mrs. Konigsmark. My crumbling self-esteem had rendered me willing to accept a romantic relationship wrapped in constant turmoil with Michaela Myers.

Everyone is worthy of unconditional love, not just the people who show up for church on Sunday morning. Until we find this special person, it is imperative to laugh about romantic hurts and failures. Laughter holds the power to heal our deepest emotional wounds. Nothing works faster to fight stress, anxiety, or emotional pain than a good laugh. Embracing humor inspires hope, builds strong interpersonal bonds, restores focus, and fortifies our minds for the challenges ahead. Laughter creates meaningful opportunities to release anger and forgive sooner. Despite all the positive benefits, though, many adults avoid moments which facilitate joy and laughter.

Here are a few practices to develop a keen sense of humor. To diffuse embarrassing situations, address failures immediately. Claim responsibility for foolish mistakes. Be the first to laugh at yourself. We are wonderfully made; embrace your imperfections. Outsiders are drawn to humor and humility. Arrogance and pride will drive people away, but humility opens the door for enduring friendships.

Humor is a powerful medicine when used properly. For example, do not crack a dirty joke at grandma's funeral to lighten the mood. Tragic events are not the best opportunities to inject humor into a painful situation. And yes, I learned this lesson the hard way, too. Suffice it to say, my grandfather's funeral was not the ideal place to drop my signature funeral home jokes, even if the place was called Crippin Funeral Home.

However, the majority of life is not filled with tragedy. Life often exists in a grey zone that presents numerous opportunities to laugh. To bring joy into our lives, we must choose laughter.

CHAPTER 8

IT WAS AWFUL

"I can't make you love me. But I can fill my pantry with your favorite
snacks and offer you a weekly stipend of $75."—Rob Delaney

NOTHING WRONG

It was the spring of 2001, and for close to three years, I had
been dating a sweet sorority sister from Georgia. The week of
graduation, she traveled to Montana to celebrate with my
family. After the twenty-four-hour celebration and a hasty
packing job, we would begin an epic, week-long road trip to
Georgia. It would include hiking the Grand Canyon, staring at
the Alamo, and watching a Brave's game in Saint Louis. At the
end of the trip, I would travel to Asia and Hawaii for several
months. When I returned in August, I would go to Florida State
University to begin a master's degree in counseling. She would
finish her senior year at the University of Georgia, then relocate
to Tallahassee. I hit the panic button when I suddenly realized
we were planning the next five years of our life together.

Looking back, there was nothing wrong with our relationship. She didn't have any weird, annoying habits, and she was

incredibly supportive. Most importantly, she had never attempted to plunge a knife into my back, though a knife wound would have been a blessing because it would have at least provided a legitimate reason to end our relationship. From my perspective, the relationship had run its course, so unbeknownst to her, I took the low road and snuck out the back door.

Allow me to back up a few weeks. There was no crazy, drunken fight at the local college bar. Her father was not being investigated by the FBI. (But maybe he should have been. She did not disclose a secret which caused our relationship to fall apart, but that could have been exciting if she had been upfront about it.)

One week before graduation, however, love was in the air, and we were at peace discussing our future plans. With zero notice, the wheels fell off. *Herbie the Love Bug* was cascading into a deep ravine, and only Superman could prevent disaster. I couldn't put my finger on exactly why, but in my heart, the relationship was over. Instead of getting ready for our road trip, I was plotting an elusive exit strategy to avoid a difficult conversation.

Being a responsible man of God, I told an extravagant lie. I would no longer need to drive to Atlanta for the Malaysia-bound flight. Delta changed the flight pattern so the first leg of the trip would begin in Seattle. (When in doubt, blame a faceless corporation.) My sister would pick up the car from the Seattle airport. Instead of returning to Seattle, I would arrive in Atlanta without the car at the end of the trip.

Nothing about the story was true. After spinning this elaborate lie, my girlfriend was shuttled onto a plane with my mother. There was one major problem—I still needed to drive to Atlanta to catch the original flight.

As this story begins to gain steam, let me repeat—I was an awful person. During the next three months of travel, I did not pick up the phone one time to call her. (Did I mention that I was an awful person?) I sent a few emails describing a five-dollar bribe I offered an immigration officer in Thailand, being asked to leave an all-you-can-eat sushi bar in Osaka, Japan, and being involved in a hit-and-run in Kuala Lumpur. I confused even myself. I was able to describe all of these mishaps in detail, but I didn't have the decency to be honest with someone I had been dating for over three years. Not the best example of Christian leadership.

It gets worse. In late August, I finally returned to Georgia after six weeks of surfing and working on a pineapple farm in Maui. Instead of calling my girlfriend after landing, I drove to Florida State to register for class. Within minutes of arriving, I discovered a major oversight. I had applied and been accepted to the wrong counseling program. I erroneously applied for a career counseling program. Counseling youth was the intended career. I have never had an interest in providing career counseling. This entire escapade was becoming as loaded with irony as an old truck crammed with junk on its way to the city dump. I was the one desperately in need of career and relationship counseling. The summer after college graduation, I enrolled in the wrong graduate program, missed the opportunity to apply for financial aid, and could not gather the courage to break up with my long-time girlfriend. Life was going way better than I could have imagined.

Instead of facing these problems head-on, I grabbed a few meager belongings and made the four-day drive to my sister's house in Portland. A few days after arriving, my sister ran into the guest bedroom, where I was sleeping on the floor, and began shouting hysterically.

"Have you seen the news?"

It was the morning of September 11th. Our country was being attacked, and I was laying in my sister's spare bedroom, drowning in a pool of misery, depression, and self-loathing. The self-inflicted torture was snowballing until I received a letter in the mail.

My Dearest Andy,

For months, I have been wondering when I would hear from you. One day we were talking about marriage. The very next day, you disappeared. I have called your father's house numerous times, and I have received no response. None of your siblings want to talk, but everyone assures me you are just fine. Thankfully, your mother finally gave me your new address in Portland. Andy, you moved to Portland without telling me.

You didn't even have the decency to tell me things were over. I have been crying for weeks on end. I did not deserve to be treated this way. I never thought you of all people were capable of such a painful conclusion to our relationship. I thought you really loved me. Instead, you ran away without a single word. I am hurt, angry, and frustrated.

In closing, I will forgive you, but I will never forget the way you treated me. We were together for three years. I deserved better than this. I thought you were better than this. I hope you enjoy your new life.

Reading that letter was like removing the world's largest band-aid made of extra strength duct tape. To this day, it remains one of the lowest moments of my life. She was right— no one deserves to be treated that way. Years later, I am still riddled with guilt over the entire experience. I never had a chance to say I was sorry, but I did not try very hard to find her. Even worse, I have never forgiven myself.

WHAT'S NEXT?

During the year living with my sister in Portland, I applied for the correct graduate program, saved money for school, and snowboarded as much as possible. To enjoy the days playing outside, I began working swing shift as a drug and alcohol counselor for teenagers. Inside the treatment facility, young patients found total security spewing venomous hatred toward anyone in their proximity. Inside this toxic environment, it is difficult to treat everyone with kindness and compassion. Patients were vindictive, manipulative, and malicious. We were verbally and physically assaulted by students on a daily basis. Not once did a student say, "Thank you for helping me turn my life around." Instead of their long-term recovery, these young men and women focused on their release dates.

A separate challenge developed between job expectations and the limitations of underqualified counselors. For example, one of our coworkers would often come to work stoned. I am not referring to stoned in the Biblical sense. No, this young lady would fire up a joint a few minutes before clocking in for her shift. She would walk into the facility reeking of marijuana. With glassy eyes, she announced, "I just need a little smoke break to help me relax at work." Yet, as a drug and alcohol counselor, she did not view this as a conflict of interest.

A different female coworker hustled for tips as an exotic dancer on her days off. Yes, the story would be spicier if a few of our male coworkers performed strip-o-grams. Instead of disrobing inside a Portland office building, the male counselors partied at the strip club after a long day counseling at the facility. These people were grown adults, but that doesn't mean they were the best role models for teenagers. Our coworker had every right to be an exotic dancer, but we might consider her desire to work as a counselor to be a conflict of interest.

The most polarizing coworker claimed to be a witch. Not

just a mean person, an actual witch. Much to my dismay, she did not cackle or have a wart on the end of her nose. She was always a good sport, never complaining about the rising cost of eye of newt. Without living the stereotypes, she claimed to be an authentic, spell-casting sorceress. Despite fears of the occult, this broom-wielding coworker was only casting benevolent spells. Hallelujah, the Lord does work in mysterious ways. Following months of intrigue, I finally said, "I think it's weird that you're a witch."

Without missing a beat, she said, "Well, I think it's weird that you're a Christian."

I thanked her for the reality check. For many, the Christian faith remains difficult to comprehend. Can I get an "amen" from the congregation? (While you're at it, slip an extra twenty in the offering plate.)

One frightful afternoon, I found the sorceress unconscious on the floor at work. She was breathing but unresponsive. Without hesitating, I grabbed the phone to call 911. After explaining the situation, the operator promised help was on the way. A flurry of activity arrived with the paramedics. Within minutes, our coworker was loaded onto the ambulance and rushed to the hospital. After a few hours in the emergency room, doctors determined she was only suffering from severe dehydration, malnourishment, and sleep deprivation. She was administered an IV and a sedative. With proper rest, our friend would be able to return to work a week later.

When she returned, everyone peppered her with questions. Her explanation was simple enough: she was physically drained after casting large quantities of spells for her sick mother. Fighting through the exhaustion, she refused to leave her beloved mother's bedside. It was necessary to cast spells until her mother was granted power over her sickness. Despite her resolve, her power was rapidly evaporating. After forty-eight excruciating hours of chanting spells, her mother was on the road to recovery. She was victorious conjuring the forces of earth, but her physical and supernatural powers were decimated.

After that bizarre ordeal, the emotional challenges of the treatment facility became too great. Students were spraying more poisonous venom than I could psychologically handle. Coworkers were abusing drugs and alcohol to cope with work pressure. Upper management was creating a toxic environment for everyone involved. Major depression was returning as life's driving force. God's love, grace and mercy had become fleeting memories. In this dark tunnel, negative thoughts were becoming a dangerous narrative.

SOMETHING HAD TO CHANGE

For the sake of my emotional health, it was time to explore a new journey. One dreary Portland afternoon in the winter of 2002, I called my friend and mentor, Chris Reny, searching for help. During my junior year of high school, I began attending Chris's youth group at Smyrna First Methodist. This fun and energetic youth pastor was everything I wanted to be when I grew up.

When we first met in the Atlanta suburbs, he was driving a lifted Jeep Wrangler and rocking a California surfer vibe. Within minutes of meeting one another, we formed an instant bond through our love for soccer, inappropriate humor and our Christian faith. Chris welcomed me into his youth group with open arms.

The church, First Methodist, became a safe haven to explore my faith. For the first time since early childhood, I felt welcome at church. Older church members never criticized my body piercings or rowdy behavior. Thankfully, Chris was creating a safe space for teenagers to ask deep questions about God.

At the end of the phone call, Chris and I had formed a new

plan. I would quit my job as a drug and alcohol counselor, pack up my meager belongings, and move to South Florida to serve as his summer youth intern. After I graduated from high school, Chris began a new position as youth pastor at First Presbyterian of Fort Lauderdale. At the end of the summer, I would move to Bozeman, Montana to begin a master's degree in the Marriage and Family Therapy program at Montana State.

CHAPTER 9

NO MORE STRIP CLUBS

"The price of success is hard work, dedication to the job at hand, and the determination that whether we win or lose, we have applied the best of ourselves to the task at hand."—Vince Lombardi

THE ZEBRA LOUNGE

In the fall of 2002, after an amazing summer serving as the youth intern at First Presbyterian of Fort Lauderdale, I re-entered the academic world. I stepped onto the Montana State campus full of hope and ambition. Despite my excitement, I had no idea how hard the challenges I would face during graduate school would be. Two years earlier, I struggled to graduate from the University of Montana. I struggled to pass a foreign language; I failed Latin and Spanish. Through determined begging and pleading, I was granted special permission to take statistics as my foreign language. Yes, statistics became my foreign language after I persuasively argued that math was a universal language. In addition to foreign languages, I struggled with English, Biology, and Calculus. As of yesterday, I still have no idea what the appropriate use of calculus is. Not once have I heard, "Oh that's just a simple calculus equation."

Finance was the one area where I did not have to struggle as an undergraduate. Our hard-working parents paid for all four Konigsmark children to go to college for four years, setting their children up for success by establishing college funds on the day we were born. Good thing our parents didn't have five kids, because numero cinco would have been cut from the college team.

During the application process for graduate school, I quickly discovered that I had zero concept of budgeting, financial planning, or student loans. Before enrolling in the first semester at Montana State, I saved fifteen thousand dollars. This financial nest egg would cover tuition, books, and a few months of living expenses. To avoid student loans, finding a flexible, well-paying job would be crucial to my academic success.

THE PLAN WENT BAD

In the first couple of weeks at Montana State, everything was falling into place. I found an affordable apartment close to campus. The Zebra Lounge, a local college bar, hired me as a poker dealer. Dealing poker can be a lucrative profession, allowing experienced dealers to earn several hundred dollars a night in tips and wages. For concerned citizens, poker is legal in Montana, but bars and restaurants must obtain an official license from the state gaming commission.

In addition to finding a place to live and a flexible part-time job, the classes and professors at Montana State were interesting and engaging. During the first month of school, I didn't have a single complaint about school, or work either, until the gaming commission shut down our illegal poker game. Everyone at the Zebra Lounge was surprised it was illegal and that they needed a state gaming license. The game was shut down, and everyone involved with it was slapped with a fine.

I was shocked by the unexpected turn of events, but I wasn't too concerned about finding another job. I knew from previous experience that flexible, part-time jobs are plentiful in college towns. As a result, I casually began searching for a decent job to cover rent, snowboarding, and Ramen noodles. With zero passion, I applied for numerous jobs, including waiting tables, dealing poker, bartending, washing dishes, and cleaning office buildings at night. Maybe I set my sights too high, or perhaps too low, but after three months of searching, I was still unemployed. Through the local temp service, I was able to pick up odd jobs a couple of days a week shoveling snow, answering phone calls, and picking up trash. These sad little jobs did not provide enough money to continue taking classes. As a result, I was financially forced to withdraw after completing just one semester of the three-year program.

Five months after beginning graduate studies at Montana State, I was financially, emotionally and spiritually broken. Without a plan for the future, life was spiraling out of control. In total frustration, God had been placed in the rearview mirror. Paying bills, buying groceries and looking for work felt like monumental tasks. Depression was clouding my judgment, and a fear of failure was holding a painful grip.

As my life moved toward a dark place, I began experiencing debilitating panic attacks. The first time it happened, I thought I was having a heart attack. My heart was racing, my ears were buzzing, and the walls were closing in. After a little bit of online research, the symptoms pointed to severe depression coupled with invasive panic attacks.

Something had to change. If I did not take control, my life was going to be ruined by mental illness. With frustration and desperation on the rise, it became my personal mission to paper

Bozeman with resumes on a daily basis. To change the tide of events, it was imperative to find a job.

As weeks became months of unemployment, friends suggested turning to the government for help. One major problem: individuals cannot file for unemployment insurance after being fired from an illegal poker game. A layman might compare this to a drug dealer filing a worker's compensation claim after being shot in a police raid.

As my bank account hit single digits, I made the decision to sell my Honda Civic. The sale netted enough money to cover rent, bills, and food for a couple of months. Now I was facing a new problem; a lack of transportation, which placed a limit on job opportunities.

A few days after selling my car, I received a phone call to interview for a full-time internship with the university's Methodist Ministry Fellowship. Finally, an actual, in-person interview after months of rejection. Things were starting to look up. The ministry director was excited to meet me after learning about my previous youth ministry experience with First Presbyterian of Fort Lauderdale.

Full of vigor, I jogged to the interview from my apartment, which was located a couple of miles from campus. Everything was moving in the right direction until the ministry director asked why I left my previous job at the Zebra Lounge.

"Well, I was dealing cards at the Zebra Lounge. Everything was great for the first month, but it turned out we were running an illegal poker game. The gaming commissioner came in one night and shut us down. I was fired and have been looking for steady work for the last couple of months. I've actually had to withdraw from classes at the university until I figure out my finances. When I saw the posting for this job, I thought we would be a perfect fit."

The director looked me in the eyes. "Andy, I would love to hire you. You have experience and passion for youth. The

Methodist Church doesn't take a hard stance against many things, but this organization is definitely against gambling. You are welcome to join our community fellowship on Wednesday nights, but at this time, we cannot consider your application for this ministry position." With this, he rose from his seat and placed a gentle hand on my shoulder. He offered a short prayer and then ushered me out the door.

CROSSING JOBS OFF THE LIST

After the ministry director's harsh rebuke, I was able to cross another job off the list. Work options were dwindling, and my spirit was shrinking after experiencing months of rejection. I landed a third interview at Wal-Mart for a job giving cars oil changes. As mentioned, during my late teens and early twenties, I worked full-time for an automotive repair shop in my hometown of Smyrna, Georgia. I'm not an expert at many things, but I have changed more oil than a fry cook at McDonalds.

After completing the third interview, the manager at Wal-Mart said, "Andy, you seem like a real nice kid, but I can't hire you for this position. I hate to say this, but you're overqualified."

I would love to see the look on my high school counselor's face if she heard I was considered overqualified for a job at Wal-Mart. In the history of the world, a customer has never filed a complaint about an overqualified employee. Just imagine this scenario, "Yeah, I would have bought a new truck today, but the salesmen really understood my budget constraints and specific vehicle needs. He wasn't pushy and spent his time making sure we found the best deal. After picking my dream truck, I became discouraged when I wasn't left with enough questions. I hate to say this, but the salesman was too knowledgeable. It's a real shame that these dealerships don't hire more idiots to sell cars."

Tossing my pride out the window, I begged the supervisor to

give me a chance. His response was firm: "I'd love to hire you, but you're going to quit the moment you get a better job."

Game over, with the final score, Wal-Mart one, Team Konigsmark zero. I lost without getting a chance to take the field. Hanging my head in shame, I shuffled out the office door. Before leaving the building, the manager began graciously pouring salt on the fresh wound, "Just call your parents! I'm sure they'll give you money."

Walking home, I kept replaying the manager's parting shot, "Just call your parents." After three humbling interviews, I was turned down for an entry level job at Wal-Mart. Here I am, a college graduate and a recent graduate school dropout being passed over for a job changing oil. Fueled by desperation, I gathered the courage to call my father for money.

"Dad, I didn't get the job at Wal-Mart. After three freaking interviews, the manager said I was overqualified. Of course, I am overqualified, but I need a job."

"Son, I read just yesterday that Coca-Cola is going to lay off 10,000 employees in the next year. It's a tough job market out there for everyone."

Not the words of encouragement I was seeking. Laying down my pride, I gathered my words. "This is really hard to ask, but I'm in a bad way. I sold my car to cover the bills for the next couple of months, but I could really use a little financial help. Nothing crazy; just a little bit of grace. Maybe a thousand dollars so I can get back on my feet."

After a few moments of total silence, I heard, "Andy, I love you too much to give you money. If I give you money today, I will be giving you money for the rest of your life."

My first thought was *I'm willing to take that risk*. In retrospect, though, I don't resent my father for this experience. True, a thousand dollars would have just been an expensive band-aid. In fact, I applaud my parents for taking the high road. Instead of sending money, they offered endless amounts of prayer, love and encouragement.

IT WAS A BAD SCENE

While I was caught in a toxic spiral of depression and despera-tion, my roommates at Montana State were punching the time clock at the local strip club. No, they were not dancers. Instead, they were paying the bills by working security at the club.

On a routine basis, sex, alcohol and drugs were following my roommates out of the strip club and into our apartment. Exotic dancers high on crystal meth would show up at all hours of the night. Late night beer pong was followed by strangers sleeping on the living room floor. Beer bottles, cigarette butts, and drug paraphernalia were scattered around the tiny apartment.

Most nights, the strip club drama did not create tension with my personal drama. Early one morning, the narrative changed when a strung-out dancer hit rock bottom in our living room. At four a.m., she burst through our front door carrying a two-year-old boy. Despite the hour, she was screaming and wailing at the top of her lungs. Startled awake, I rushed downstairs, rubbing sleep out of my eyes. Without saying a word, she thrust the toddler into my arms and ran out the front door.

Without collecting $200 for passing Go, I had been entrusted to take care of an unknown toddler. For the sake of the child, I wasn't going to call the police or child protective services. I didn't want this little boy to end up in the system without his mother. I frantically began calling every number I could think of to find the child's closest relative. By mid-after-noon, I located his grandmother, who lived a couple hours away. Without asking too many questions, she arrived later in the evening to take him home.

I have no idea what happened to the child after he left our apartment that day, but I am certain I made the best decision for all parties involved. I can't imagine the mother's pain when she thrust her child into a stranger's arms. She must have believed she was making the best possible decision for her child with the resources available to her. These were not the moments I was expecting during graduate school. No one should encounter these issues, but that is not the world in which we live. Therefore, it is our calling to remain present in difficult situations. Despite this invasive wake-up call, I refused to ask the outside world for help. I was cognizant that life had become emotionally unstable, but I could not afford health insurance, anti-depressants, or professional help. A dark cloud of depression was swirling into all aspects of life. I needed help but refused to seek support or guidance from a local church. Since childhood, meditative prayer kept my spirit aligned with God, yet I stubbornly ignored prayer as a gateway to personal freedom. Lacking proper direction, I was creating a personal version of hell on earth. As hopelessness continued to rise, the teachings of Jesus Christ were being pushed further into the back of my mind. I was running from Christianity in a shallow effort to absolve immense feelings of guilt and shame. The plan had gone bad, and I was unsure how to pull out of the tailspin.

I FOUND WORK

The financial cushion I had created by selling my car was almost gone. Something had to change. Within a few short weeks, my checking account would be completely empty. I had no prospects for a loan and nothing of value left to sell. This may sound extreme, but living on the streets and begging for food and money didn't seem crazy. I couldn't imagine my situation becoming more desperate.

Waking from a haze of depression, a lifeline finally arrived on a subzero Montana morning. A local plumbing company called to offer a job. The pipes in a brand-new home had burst, filling the first floor and basement with icy cold water. To prevent mold and further water damage, the house would have to be drained and gutted. The company asked if I would be willing to tackle the cold, wet, miserable job. Without hesitation, I answered yes. I did not question how much I would be paid or the hours required. For the first time in months, except for being offered a job flipping burgers at the strip club, I was being offered full-time work. This lily pad opportunity would provide enough financial security until I was ready to leap to the next stage of life.

The first day of work, I walked outside and was rudely greeted with weather of minus forty degrees. I spit to see if it's true that it freezes in midair before hitting the ground if the air is cold enough. It is. (Before you pass this idea off as complete nonsense, make sure you try it at least once.)

When temperatures drop this low, you long for hot, humid summer nights filled with cockroaches, pit stains, and sweltering porta potties. Subzero temperatures wreaked havoc on my emotions and the dilapidated work van. After exhausting every G-rated cussword I could muster, the engine squealed to life, priming the carburetor for twenty frustrating minutes. Shivering in the driver's seat, I made the thirty-minute drive to the frozen tundra known as Livingston, Montana.

By the time I arrived, water was seeping out the front door and gushing from the basement windows. Filled with trepidation, I slowly opened the door. There was no tidal wave cascading down the stairs, but the first floor was filled with several feet of freezing cold water. Surveying the damage, it was apparent a wetsuit would be the most appropriate attire. However, no scuba gear was available, so I stripped down to my tighty-whities and began schlepping hoses and pumps into the house. As the pumps furiously sucked from the house, I systematically ripped apart drywall, carpet, and hardwood flooring. This would be my job for the next couple of weeks, until all of the water was removed.

MISERY

After a month of cold, wet and lonely work, I was physically and emotionally broken. Yes, I had food and money to pay the bills. A steady job was providing much needed structure, but life was not improving. Crying myself to sleep on an inflatable mattress could not remove the pain. I had reached the end of my rope. I did not want to live another day. With great apprehension, I got on my knees and began crying out to God. Sobbing, I mustered the solemn words, "God, I don't want it anymore. You can have my life. I will do anything. I will go anywhere. Just take away the pain." After crying out, I quietly listened for guidance from the Divine. Within the evangelical tradition, these moments are called fleecing God. This type of fleecing does not include stealing from God in an elaborate Ponzi scheme. Instead, we are hustling or pleading for the Almighty to make our decisions.

The idea of fleecing God begins with Gideon in the Book of Judges. God commands Gideon to attack the Midianites who have invaded the struggling country of Israel. To overthrow the enemy invaders, God sends a messenger to Gideon. "Go with your strength and save Israel from the Midianites." (Judges 6:14)

Despite the message from God, Gideon refuses to attack the Midianites. Instead, he asks God for a miracle. In the first reported miracle, a fire consumes Gideon's dinner offering. But this miracle was not enough to convince Gideon to lead his people into a bloody revolution. Ignoring God's first miracle, Gideon lays a sheepskin on the ground to challenge God, saying he will only go to war if the morning presents a wet fleece surrounded by dry ground. It's a pretty bold move, but God rises to the challenge. Gideon, acting like an insufferable teenager, asks God for a third miracle. This time, he wants the ground to be wet, but the fleece must remain dry. Again, God rises to the test. After losing his sheepskin challenges, Gideon gathers the people to make war against the Midianites. Thanks to Gideon, rebellious adults have been calling on this story to fleece the will of God for thousands of years.

After a tortuous night searching for anything made from sheepskin, an unexpected phone call lifted my spirits. Like manna from heaven, Chris Reny, my childhood youth pastor, called to offer spiritual, emotional, and financial support. For the second time in less than a year, he offered an exit strategy.

Chris said, "Andy, just pack up your stuff and come back to Fort Lauderdale. We will figure this out. I'm sure we can find you a job if the church can't afford to bring you on staff for the summer."

Approximately a year earlier, in the spring of 2002, Chris saved me from a soul-sucking year working as a drug and alcohol counselor in Oregon. Now, in the summer of 2003, I would return to South Florida for the second summer in a row. I would serve as the youth intern at First Presbyterian of Fort Lauderdale until I was able to land a full-time youth ministry job.

Tucking my tail between my legs, I bid my roommates, the plumbing company, and girlfriend adieu. The roommates were stoic with the sudden turn of events, the plumber was frustrated, and the girlfriend was stunned. She suffered betrayal. She was filled with anger. She had been deceived. One moment everything was fine, and the next I was leaving town. There is no excuse for my deplorable behavior. I know I was not living as the best version of myself, but I should not have jerked the rug out from underneath the poor woman.

In desperation, she offered to quit school and move to Florida to pursue ministry together. It was a sweet offer, but an offer I could not entertain. The challenge—ministry—was my calling, not hers. From my perspective, we were on separate journeys, and I had reached a fork in the road. Full of shame, I explained that I was taking a new path that did not include her. The breakup was painful, but the guilt was worse; long-standing guilt that was formed during my conservative Christian upbringing.

Needing to make a quick exit, I scraped together enough money to purchase a 1987 Honda Civic with over 300,000 miles on the odometer. The car didn't come with air-conditioning or a passenger's side mirror, but it had four tires and enough life to get past the Montana border. Wasting little time, I stuffed a few meager belongings into the hatchback and began the three-day trek back to Florida.

My first year of graduate school was not the success story I had envisioned. Less than twelve months after spending an energizing summer with my friend and mentor, depression, anxiety, and loneliness were returning as the driving forces of my life. Needing to restore my soul, I ran toward safety. For the second time, Chris Reny and his church were offering a new beginning. Before arriving, the church graciously offered to cover all of my travel expenses for the long drive from Montana to Florida. And again, the Yianilos family offered to share a spare bedroom in their beautiful home. Everything was falling into place. This hot mess of a life was transforming into an unexpected spiritual journey.

IT'S A CALLING

For the second consecutive summer, I returned to serve as the summer youth intern for First Presbyterian of Fort Lauderdale. The church offered a steady paycheck and a free place to live until I was able to land a full-time youth ministry job. Before the summer of 2003, I had never envisioned ministry as my calling in life. From an early age, I have been known as a

Christian, but I had never felt called by God to serve the church.

In high school, I was voted "most spirited," which is a nice term for most hyper. No one would have guessed I would have been called into the ministry. I was destined to be an auto mechanic, not an ordained minister.

Throughout college, I had been aimlessly bouncing around without a solid plan. I was being guided by a fear of failure rather than a desire to shine. I approached life counting mile markers instead of remaining open to the journey ahead.

Becoming an ordained minister has to be more than a job description. Yes, anyone can become a minister, but not everyone who loves God should enter the ministry. The clergy becomes watered down when men and women treat ministry as a fall back plan. Being a minister is who you are, it's not a time-card you can punch. It is a powerful calling when an individual gives up something to pursue full-time ministry. Successful clergy members hold the necessary skills to excel in a different profession, vocation, or opportunity. As a result, passionate ministers do not need the church; a congregation needs them.

CHAPTER 10

CHURCH OF THE BIG WOOD

"To be a minister means, above all, to become powerless, or in more precise terms, to speak with our powerlessness to the condition of powerlessness which is so keenly felt but so seldom expressed by the people of our age."—Henri Nouwen

WHAT'S WRONG WITH THE NAME?

In the fall of 2003, after five months interning with First Presbyterian of Fort Lauderdale, I began serving as the youth pastor for the Presbyterian Church of The Big Wood. Despite the name, there is no official connection with the adult film industry. With proper marketing, we could have developed a creative sponsorship from Viagra. The retired NASCAR driver, Dick Trickle, turned down our requests to serve as church ambassador. Just imagine the marketing campaign behind "Have your spirits lifted with Church of The Big Wood." Yes, it is a Christian church with a funny name. These ideas caused some high school students to call me the world's worst youth pastor. But I didn't mind. Someone has to be the world's worst youth pastor.

In my defense, I have never insisted on dunking Oreos in milk while taking communion.

After being hired, I asked the senior pastor, "Do you find the name of the church funny?"

He promptly explained the church was located on the Big Wood River, and that only people with their minds in the gutter would find humor in the name. Our small group of locals might be the only people in America without their minds in the gutter. I understand geography, but we must create space to laugh at ourselves.

One day at a staff meeting, I suggested we remove Big Wood from the side of the bus. I was hoping for something a little less punchline-worthy. To support my argument, we called my father on the speakerphone.

"Dad, when you hear *Big Wood*, what do you think of?"

Without missing a beat, my father replied, "Well, son, I think of a huge (expletive)..."

To save further embarrassment, I dove across the conference table to hit the "end call" button but missed it. As I was fumbling with the buttons, everyone heard, "You tell those church people that after the prostate cancer, I was scared I would never return to the Church of the Big Wood, if you know what I mean."

"Yes, Dad, we all know what you mean."

Because of my father's subtle prompt, the church granted permission to remove all signage from the youth van. High school is hard enough; we didn't need a van with a funny name. On previous road trips, strangers would stop the van to take photos. Everyone was laughing except members of the congregation. The answer was always the same: "There is nothing funny about the Big Wood River. We are proud of our heritage." I agreed there was nothing wrong with our heritage, but there might be something wrong with our advertising campaign.

THE PURITY MOVEMENT

When I first became a youth minister, the evangelical purity movement was reigning supreme for Christian youth. The message was clear—sex outside of marriage dishonors God. Our sexuality is a gift meant to be shared between a husband and wife. As teenage hormones were raging, youth ministers across the country were reminding students to remain pure. Sex is dangerous. Lustful thoughts are disgraceful. Christians must avoid all forms of sexual temptation. I became caught up in the purity movement and found myself unable to foster healthy conversations about sex. When confronted with a sexual roadblock, I would urge students to remain pure.

Teens across America were becoming emotionally and sexually paralyzed by the leaders of the purity movement. Christian leaders were capitalizing on sexual fear. In the cult classic *Mean Girls,* Coach Carr reminds high school students, "Don't have sex, because you will get pregnant and die! Don't have sex in the missionary position, don't have sex standing up, just don't do it, okay? Promise? Okay, now everybody take some rubbers."

This is some of the same ridiculous advice being perpetrated by naïve Christian leaders, except the majority of churches across America would never talk to children about safe sex.

Students were falsely believing they would get pregnant, contract a sexually-transmitted disease, and become unlovable the first time they had sex before marriage. Sex within the confines of marriage was placed on an unreachable pedestal. Little to no grace was offered for students engaging in premarital sex.

In my circle of influence, no one was considering healthy conversations regarding sexuality. Everything regarding sex was forbidden until marriage. A dangerous message was gaining traction—if Christian teens are able to remain pure until marriage, the floodgates of sexual fulfillment would burst open. On the other hand, if teens have sex before marriage, they will follow a dark road to sexual disappointment.

Despite my belief that churches and ministers need to lead their congregations in healthy conversations about sexuality, I was unequipped to lead these necessary conversations. Furthermore, zero progressive discussions were taking place to discuss students who identify with the LGBTQ community. From a mainstream, evangelical perspective, a heterosexual marriage is the only way to honor God. In Joshua Harris's book *I Kissed Dating Goodbye*—a must-read—within the purity movement, students are encouraged to marry as soon as possible. As a result, heterosexual marriage is the avenue to avoid premarital sex rather than a path for creating a loving and fulfilling partnership.

As a single youth minister, I was struggling to understand my sexuality. Just like the teens I was serving, a constant battle to understand love, intimacy and dating was taking place. The entire conversation regarding sex was hidden behind layers of guilt, shame, and secrecy. So, instead of embracing the unknown, I was putting sex on a pedestal. For the majority of young adults, waiting until marriage has become an outdated and antiquated concept.

After a youth conference, one of the teens in our group said, "Abstinence is so 1820's. Andy, only idiots like you are trying to save themselves for marriage."

This was not the first nor last time I was confronted with this argument. The church, and I, in my own way, have done a poor job exploring human sexuality. Instead of addressing the elephant in the room, Christians are allowing outsiders to dictate their conversations regarding sex. To create change, Christian leaders must empower future generations to make informed decisions regarding sexuality.

WORST ADVICE

During my first year of full-time youth ministry, an eighteen-year-old student came seeking advice regarding sex and marriage. To avoid sexual guilt and shame, he was planning to marry his seventeen-year-old girlfriend. For this young couple, marriage had become the gateway for guilt-free sex. It didn't take me long to respond.

"Jason, that is one of the dumbest things I have heard in a long time. You don't get married to your high school girlfriend just to have sex. Please listen carefully because I am about to give you terrible advice. Marriage is more than sex. If you want to have sex that badly, I'll buy you condoms, or we will find someone to help your girlfriend get on birth control but do not get married to have sex."

This unfiltered statement could lead to negative consequences, but I refused to encourage two teenagers to get married so they could have sex. Unfortunately, this young couple did not listen to my anti-Purity Movement advice. An older pastor within our community was more than willing to perform a wedding ceremony, thus saving this young couple from further sexual temptation. A few short weeks after graduating high school, with their parents' blessings, the couple were blissfully walking down the aisle together. To no one's surprise, I was not invited to the celebration. With limited finances, the newlyweds moved into Jason's childhood bedroom. To support his new family, the husband began working for his father's construction company. The wife stayed at home to help around the house.

Think about this for a moment—a month earlier, this couple was pulling all-nighters to study for high school exams. But instead of planning for college, they were having sex, playing video games, and spending their first weeks of marriage sharing a bathroom with his younger siblings.

Before celebrating their first anniversary, the teenage couple became first-time parents. Two years later, they welcomed a little girl into their family. By age twenty-five, the couple had four children and were still living with his parents. After eight years, the wife filed for divorce, claiming she had been forced into the marriage. At the tender age of twenty-seven, the young woman and her four children moved back home with her parents.

This is not intended to be an "I told you so" story, but rather a word of caution. Marriage should not be a plan for escape, but an opportunity to create something beautiful.

RECKLESS GOLF CARTING

During the years serving Church of the Big Wood, I was invited on an annual basis to function as youth speaker for a nearby Presbyterian summer camp. A few weeks before leaving for camp, I endured the second of four anterior cruciate ligament surgeries. As I was recovering from surgery, the camp director graciously offered the official Camp Sawtooth golf cart to help navigate the distances between venues. Despite the unfortunate circumstance, my soul was gently lifted while zipping past disinterested high school students.

As I recall, it was a beautiful summer afternoon in the Sawtooth Mountains when the golf cart accidentally damaged some camp benches. Well, not so much an accident, because the junior counselor grabbed the wheel and we rammed them, laughing hysterically the whole time. In our defense, these one-hundred-year-old wooden benches should have been able to handle a high-speed attack from an electric vehicle. Instead, we came to an abrupt stop amid a sea of wooden fragments. Being responsible adults, we gathered the broken pieces and deceptively hid them in a discreet woodpile.

At the evening campfire, the camp director pulled me aside, and with a concerned look on her face, asked, "Andy, is there anything you want to tell me?"

There I was, a twenty-seven-year-old man, afraid to answer the camp director. With as much courage as I could muster, I said, "Nothing you don't already know."

At this point, I thought for sure I was busted. She responded, "I just wanted to make sure there are no announcements we need to make for the morning. Also, it was a pleasure having you serve at camp this summer."

There was no harm-no foul until the director began addressing the students that evening.

"I hope everyone had a great day. But before Andy comes and speaks with you tonight, we need to take care of a little housekeeping. I believe someone in our group has broken a few items. I don't want to point fingers, but I am certain the responsible individuals will come forward to admit their guilt."

Naturally, all of the campers began looking around for the guilty party. With a little bit of luck, maybe some innocent teenager would take the blame just to impress the cute girl sitting in the front row. Dangit, no such luck. Looking to take the high road, I snuck back to my golf cart of shame to find a couple of benches to attack before leaving camp in the morning.

I WORK MORE THAN SUNDAYS

A few months before the reckless golf cart excursion, a sweet young couple from church asked if I would perform their wedding. Caught off-guard by the invitation, I politely declined. This decision proved correct, until the senior minister got word. At our next staff meeting, he said, "Great job, everyone. Oh, one more thing—Andy, you will be performing the wedding for that young couple."

Being a young, single minister, I didn't know the first thing about weddings. I didn't know any of the etiquette for bouquets, exchanging vows, or giving rings. I didn't want to be responsible for ruining the happiest day of some poor couple's life. I was petrified from the moment the ceremony began until I said, "You may kiss the bride."

I was feeling pretty good about my effort until the maid of honor asked, "Did you become a youth minister because you failed at everything else in life?"

Being a thoughtful person, I responded, "This may come as a surprise, but I never wanted to be a minister. Matter of fact, as a child, I dreamed of growing up to become a dog. It wasn't until I contracted a deadly case of heartworm that I began to consider a career change."

With a solid stink-face, the fair young maiden turned on her heels and walked away in search of someone else to offend.

Before becoming a full-time youth pastor, no one in my circle of trust thought it would be helpful to explain the upcoming challenges. Youth ministers are inherently underpaid and overworked. They do not punch a timecard to start and finish the workday. Parents call at the crack of dawn to discuss issues their high school students are experiencing with siblings, home life, and peer relationships. Parents are not calling for emotional support; they expect the local youth pastor to fix all of their children's problems.

After students finish school for the day, they call and text way past midnight to discuss their personal problems. Let's not forget the crusty old church members refusing to acknowledge the importance of youth ministry. Most outsiders do not realize the best youth workers are clocking over sixty hours a week and fueling their bodies on church leftovers. Being a youth minister is much more than Sunday night youth group, summer camp, and attending basketball games. They're immersed in teenage problems that older adults deem insignificant.

Without proper training, ministers of all kinds are constantly balancing work and theological politics. Seminary does not prepare students for the critics who vigorously search for every opportunity to point out perceived flaws and shortcomings. Conversely, ministry advocates often remain hidden during the darkest hours of need. Without warning, all personal time is subject to individual attack. Too often, churches hold the reigns of their ministers too tightly. As church members battle for control, leadership within the church begins to break down.

Despite the challenges facing our ministers, youth ministers can succeed by embracing a spirit of humility. Successful leaders must be filled with passion for empowering teenagers, especially teens who are struggling to understand the Christian faith in an evolving post-Christian culture. Despite what evangelical culture teaches our youth, the world is changing. To remain relevant and vibrant, Christianity must evolve, too.

To foster longevity in an under-appreciated profession, sacrifices are necessary. This includes embracing a pitiful paycheck to cover repairs on a used minivan. On the best days, deep fried food, concession stand nachos, and energy drinks will serve as improper nourishment to make it through the afternoon. No one seems to care about the underpaid youth worker who spends extra money attending high school musicals, having coffee dates, and purchasing water guns. For anyone struggling to chase a dream, it is imperative to embrace the journey. Often, the fruits of ministry only begin to appear years later.

Many people outside the church do not understand a minister's role within the local community. "You have the easiest job in the world; you only have to work one day a week," they say. However, the six days leading up to Sunday morning worship are the most time-consuming. During the week, ministers are preparing for Sunday service, counseling church members, organizing the budget, planning mission trips, building community relations, assisting with Children's Church, providing counseling, facilitating long-term plans for growth, and a thousand other random jobs no one cares to mention. With proper dedication, the calling will be rewarding, but there is always work to be done.

CHAPTER 11

I LEFT A GOOD THING

"I don't mind how much my ministers talk, as long as they do what I say."—Margaret Thatcher

AFTER THE DAMAGE . . .

After breaking the benches and two short years serving the students in Sun Valley, I found myself being called to attend Fuller Seminary. In the moment, I could not explain the rationale for the decision. I was actively enjoying my job, church, and community. Thus, the decision to resign came as a surprise to many. Big Wood was loving, thoughtful and supportive. From an outsider's perspective, there was no reasonable explanation for relocating to California. I was financially secure, enjoying the outdoors, and the senior minister was a tremendous mentor. Despite reaching a sweet spot in life, though, my restless soul was confronting an indiscernible urge to change my life's trajectory.

In August of 2005, I left the Church of the Big Wood with great trepidation to pursue a Master of Divinity through Fuller Seminary. It was early on a cold Idaho morning when I finished loading my truck. Anything that didn't fit in the bed was given to the Gold Mine, a local thrift shop. The sun was cresting over the mountains as I pulled away. During the fourteen-hour drive, regret filled every nook and cranny of my heart. After crossing the California border, I told myself, "Andy, it's too late to turn around. You can do this. You were made for this." The pep talk did little to improve my mood, but it was too late to change my mind. Now, the only thing to do was create a new path and stop looking backward.

EVERYTHING CHANGED

Thirty minutes before reaching my new apartment in Pasadena, a little girl in our neighborhood had been shot and killed during a gang fight. It was complete chaos in the streets as I was searching for a parking space. The block was swarming with activity. Dozens of police officers were combing the streets and alleys and interviewing bystanders. Multiple helicopters casting high-beam spotlights were circling overhead. Twenty-four hours earlier, I was enjoying the serenity of an Idaho sunset; now violence from the outside world was closing in. Feelings of extreme anxiety and regret began filling my every pore.

After circling the block for over half an hour, I squeezed my truck into a miniscule parking space near my new apartment. Hesitating to take my hands off the ignition, I kept asking myself, "What have I done?" My hands tightly gripped the keys, and fear was telling me to turn around. Questions were flooding my brain. Was it too late to cry uncle and return to Idaho? If I returned, would Church of the Big Wood begin shouting, "Hosanna, Hosanna in the highest"? Maybe this was a terrible mistake.

Despite the uncertainty of life and the cascading flood of emotions, I knew it was too late to turn around. Full of apprehension, I hustled to the front gate and used the call box to ask my new roommates for help. Wasting no time, they jogged through the security gates to help me unload. In less than ten minutes, my pitiful possessions were carried inside. In our run-down neighborhood, everything was susceptible to theft.

Still in shock, I walked into our gloomy apartment, and we unceremoniously dumped all my worldly possessions onto the dingy bedroom floor. Intense anxiety created a wave of nausea in my body. Feelings of loneliness were rising, and I was too proud to call anyone to ask for help. As a twenty-seven-year-old man, it was time to put down the sippy cup and use a big boy cup.

With little direction, I began searching for the inflatable mattress. As I began inflating it, one of my roommates knocked on the door. "Andy, I know you just arrived, but I wanted to invite you to watch *The Exorcism of Emily Rose.*"

How could I possibly go watch a movie about exorcism? I had reached my emotional breaking point. Within moments, the tears would be streaming down my face. An innocent little girl had just been killed right outside the front door. I couldn't justify paying money to watch a movie about evil when our neighborhood was frantically searching for a killer.

Tears filled my eyes as the helicopter illuminated the second-hand furniture in our unfamiliar apartment. Instead of making conversation with my new roommates, I crawled onto the inflatable mattress and wrapped a blanket tightly around my body. The first night in California was worse than I could have imagined.

JESUS LOVES PORN STARS

Before walking onto Fuller's campus for orientation in the fall of 2005, I had formed very few opinions about seminary. In an attempt to identify like-minded students at new student orientation, I selected a hot pink T-shirt with *Jesus loves porn stars* emblazoned across the front. The shirt was produced by a progressive Christian ministry called XXX Church; an organization which supports men and women whose lives are being impacted by the adult entertainment industry. Minutes after walking into the auditorium, I was approached by a young lady with tears streaming down her face. Caught off-guard, I asked, "What's wrong?"

Between sobs, she said, "Why would you wear that?"

"Are you talking about this shirt, or these sad shorts I should have retired two years ago?"

Choking back tears, she asked, "Why would you wear a shirt about Jesus loving porn stars to seminary?"

"I know the message might not be popular, but this ministry is helping men and women escape the porn industry. Too often, we forget that Jesus came for the marginalized, the broken, and people who work in the porn industry."

Looking back, I should have worn my *Dukes of Hazzard* shirt, but it was dirty from the gym. The *Jesus loves porn stars* shirt was designed to make a statement, but I was not looking to rattle the cages of conservative classmates.

I want to be known as a forward-thinking, inclusive Christian but I still need to be reminded that Jesus loved the prostitutes, the tax collectors, the cheats. He loved the people we push to the outskirts of society. As seminary students, we must remain focused on the ministry at hand.

Here's the point—many people within the evangelical tradition want Jesus to play favorites. In this short-sighted worldview, Jesus is an American citizen who supports their political views and speaks fluent English. For many, it is morally offensive to proclaim Jesus's love for crack dealers. He does not support their actions, but he loves the spiritually wounded person struggling to make sense of this fragile world. As we dig deeper into Christian tradition, we understand Jesus does not side with Democrats or Republicans. The Son of God did not come to earth to enforce political agendas. Instead, Jesus came into this world to understand and suffer with the people. His heart breaks for the men and women existing in a constant state of oppression.

LITTLE TIMMY JOHNSON

There's no doubt about it—Fuller Seminary is filled with unique personalities anxiously searching for the perfect moment to share their awkward journey of faith. There is no popular crowd making all the rules. Bullies, drug dealers and fraternity parties do not exist. Many peers were raised within conservative Christian families; their idea of fun is drinking craft beers after class and debating theology. Other students embrace their evangelical roots by blasting Christian rap music.

During my three years attending Fuller, I encountered numerous students trying to impress everyone with their vast knowledge of the Christian tradition. As a reminder, no one really cares what little Timmy Johnson learned at Calvin College during his freshman year. We are paying thousands of dollars in tuition to reap the benefits from our current professors. Even the seminary professors do not want to hear the regurgitation of information. "If you're not happy, Timmy, you can go back to Iowa and tell grandma about the mean seminary student in your Greek class. While I am sitting in class, please stop trying to impress that girl with the one thousand verses of Scripture you have memorized. She is not impressed with your dedication to read the Bible cover-to-cover four times a year. Just remember the words of Proverbs 3:34, 'The Lord mocks the mockers but is gracious to the humble.'"

Before enrolling in seminary, I should have exercised the demons of conservative evangelical Christianity. Seminary is known as a Christian institution that prepares men and women for full-time ministry positions. Fuller Seminary, where I attended, prepares students of diverse backgrounds to serve as counselors, psychologists, and church leaders. As America's Christian culture continues to evolve, more than half of Fuller's graduates will pursue vocations outside of the church. Today, thousands of alumni serve in a variety of professional roles, including movie production, web development, fashion design, and working on Wall Street. As a result, the institution prides itself on blending art, culture and Christian tradition.

Christian high school followed by Christian college prepares thousands of students to flourish in seminary. I was raised in a Southern Baptist home but did not receive a degree from a Christian college. As a result, I spent the majority of my early twenties living outside the conservative Christian bubble. Early mornings were fueled by energy drinks rather than prayer. Trashy New York Times best-sellers replaced a desire for the New Testament. Instead of studying the words of Jesus, I watched vast amounts of professional sports. In Montana, I was dealing poker into the early hours of Sunday morning and then sleeping through worship service. As a result, I entered semi- nary lacking a deep appreciation for the Christian faith.

A haphazard high school and meandering college career did not create a recipe for long-term academic success. As a result, I entered graduate school unprepared for the numerous spiritual and academic challenges. During an exegesis class, the professor asked students to diagram a Greek sentence. After class, I politely informed our professor that I had no idea how to diagram a sentence. She was stunned that a college graduate did not understand how to identify an adverb or pronoun. Thank God, she took pity on me. Every day after class, I would study the basic concepts of English and grammar. There I was, a college graduate, being asked to relearn basic elementary school concepts at the age of twenty-nine.

Academic success would have been impossible without the support I received from Fuller's access services. Through an extensive series of tests and interviews, my learning disabilities were properly diagnosed and confronted. As a result, I was granted extended time on tests and papers. A terrific notetaker volunteered to help decode my pitiful lecture notes. Professors were empathetic to my plight and extended an abundance of love, grace and emotional support. It was a team effort to reach the finish line, but after three years of hard work, I graduated from Fuller Seminary with honors.

CHRISTIANITY IS MORE THAN A SPORTS CAR

During the first semester at Fuller, a professor asked, "Andy, do you think the universal church exists on earth even without Jesus?"

A silence fell over the classroom. I answered, "Well, if you've got a '69 Camaro, and it doesn't have an engine, it's still a '69 Camaro. It just doesn't run."

Our professor was caught off-guard by this strange response. He asked, "Did you just compare the universal church to a '69 Camaro without an engine?"

Comparing the church to a Chevrolet Camaro might seem strange, but it was a metaphor I could understand. Not wanting to challenge our professor or embarrass myself, I responded, "If the church is the vehicle for Christianity, then Jesus is the engine we should be reinstalling in the '69 Camaro. For argument's sake, Jesus would be a DZ302, one of the best motors Chevrolet ever made. The car does not need to be a convertible or have racing stripes. A hard top with a little bit of primer is perfect. As long as we remember that a '69 Camaro without an engine is still a '69 Camaro. It's just waiting for a motor."

Everyone might have been a little bit confused, at which point the professor asked, "Andy, where'd you come from?"

I said, "Georgia."

He responded, "Sounds about right."

In a desire to understand the evolving post-Christian worldview, I started seeking an understanding of Scripture in a modern context. For example, *The Parable of the Workers in the Vineyard* is a powerful story which transcends time and culture. Jesus shares the parable in Matthew 20:1-16—"For the kingdom of heaven is like the landowner who went out early one morning to hire workers for his vineyard." He agreed to pay the normal daily wage and sent them out to work. At nine o'clock in the morning, he was passing through the marketplace and saw some people standing around doing nothing. So, he hired them, telling them he would pay them whatever was right at the end of the day. They went to work in the vineyard. At noon and again at three o'clock, he did the same thing. At five o'clock that afternoon, he was in town again and saw some more people standing around. He asked them, "Why haven't you been working today?"

They replied, "Because no one hired us."

The landowner told them, "Then go out and join the others in my vineyard."

That evening, he told the foreman to call the workers in and pay them, beginning with the last workers first. When those hired at five o'clock were paid, each received a full day's wage. When those hired first came to get their pay, they assumed they would receive more. But they, too, were paid a day's wage. When they received their pay, they protested to the owner, "Those people worked only one hour, and yet you've paid them just as much as you paid us who worked all day in the scorching heat."

He answered one of them, "Friend, I haven't been unfair! Didn't you agree to work all day for the usual wage? Take your money and go. I wanted to pay this last worker the same as you. Is it against the law for me to do what I want with my money? Should you be jealous because I am kind to others?"

The same professor asked, "Andy, what do you think of this

parable?" Before forming an eloquent response, I said, "Well, I see it like those guys outside of Home Depot. They show up early every morning looking for work. Before the sun even rises, they are waiting for the kindness of a stranger. We can't blame the guys for not getting picked up for a job any more than we can blame a first-grader for being the last player chosen for dodgeball. Every one of these men shows up willing and ready to work. Their lunch is packed, and they are ready to work when the first construction trucks arrive. I don't think we should blame these able-bodied men for not being offered a job."

With tears streaming down her face, the professor said, "That's such a beautiful illustration of the migrant workers. These poor day laborers are outside of our society like the laborers in the parable. How did you pick them?"

"Pretty simple," I said, "I was trying to think of a place where I could go pick up workers for the day. The only place I could think of was Home Depot."

In the Christian tradition, we are often caught looking for deeper answers and bypassing the foundational teachings of Jesus, but sometimes, for simple needs, we must search for simple answers.

I didn't enter seminary with a strong theological foundation. During the first semester, our Old Testament professor was lecturing on the first five books of the Bible. These books are known as the Pentateuch and are often attributed to Moses. Beginning with the first book of the Bible, Genesis, he asked our class this question, "Have you ever considered the possibility that Adam and Eve weren't real people?"

I thought to myself, "Nope, never considered that." There was no room in our Southern Baptist tradition to discuss authenticity of the Creation narrative. At First Mega Church, the people who dared to challenge the authority of Scripture were labeled as heretics.

Our professor was not trying to force his beliefs upon the class. He said, "I believe Adam and Eve were created by our spiritual ancestors as an origin story. This beautiful allegory seeks to understand the creation of humans. It was not written as a factual account. Instead, it offers an explanation about the relationship between God and humans."

For the first time in my life, I began to consider Adam and Eve as literary characters created by our ancient spiritual brothers. Seminary professors encourage students to search for deeper meanings within the pages of Scripture. Our faith should not crumble if Adam and Eve are literary characters created by the author(s) of Genesis. Making sense of a confusing world is the central theme of the creation story. Unfortunately, in the conservative tradition in which I was raised, it was foundational to believe Adam and Eve were historic figures. Furthermore, it was imperative to blame Satan, disguised as a snake, for deceiving the first humans.

In stark contrast to my conservative Christian upbringing, our Old Testament professor said, "It's more powerful to think about these early people sitting around a campfire discussing their existence. The people were forcing themselves to make sense of a good God who rewarded the faithful, at the same time questioning the wrath and punishment of God."

By embracing the professor's perspective, a deeper appreciation for the creation story can begin to form. Throughout the Old Testament, the people are trying to make sense of their broken world. In the New Testament, we find people approaching Jesus with similar concerns. Jesus was asked, "What sins has this man or his family committed so that he has this affliction?" Jesus replied, "This man has no sins." Yet we want to believe bad things happen to bad people; this is our version of justice. The world is not fair, but we continue to believe God is going to reward us for our good deeds. In turn, we assume God is going to punish people for doing evil. But that's not what we read in Scripture; according to Jesus, people do not receive physical afflictions because of some grievous sin or mistake they have committed. Unfortunately, pain, suffering and disease exist outside the kingdom of heaven.

More Degrees than a Burnt Piece of Chicken

Fifteen years after being told I would be lucky to graduate high school, I graduated Fuller Seminary with a Master of Divinity. With degree in hand, I was ready to conquer the giant world of ministry. There was only one small problem. After three intense years of studying to be a minister, I finished school with a large amount of debt and no idea how to perform the actual functions of being a minister. Seminary trains students for ministry, but no amount of classroom education can prepare graduates to express their love of God when a five-year-old child has been diagnosed with terminal cancer.

Seminary creates theological leaders, but many professors are incapable of preparing students for the challenges of ministry. A one-day seminar called *Church Politics: Dealing with Angry Church Members* would have been extremely helpful. Setting aside thirty minutes would have been beneficial to teach students healthy options for antagonistic mothers carrying a personal vendetta (not that I'm speaking from personal experience). Church finances are also a constant struggle for ministers serving in small churches, but the seminary did not mention this challenge either. When I become a seminary professor, I will offer a class titled *No One Respects the Local Minister, Except His Mama.*

It is important to understand that a seminary education will not provide all the answers. A class designed to practice weddings, baptisms and funerals would be helpful, but these types of classes are not a part of the traditional seminary curriculum. In life, we often have to fake it until we make it. Do not discount the power of presence. Often, showing up in difficult situations will generate perfect opportunities to share the love of God. Therefore, getting our hands dirty is essential for fulfilling a lifetime of ministry serving God.

Here's the point—a formal education cannot provide the difficult answers for a pregnant fifteen-year-old girl, yet this young girl needs someone who will listen and love without judgment. In these unpredictable moments, God is glorified.

DAVID

To pay the bills in seminary, I worked for a covert catering company, The Pasadena Kitchen. Seriously, TPK must have been owned and operated by a former CIA informant. The company refused to advertise and only employed known assets. On Wednesday evenings, our elite force of food delivery specialists would receive an encrypted email with the current work assignment. It was our mission if we chose to accept.

The first email I received from the company said, "Wear all black. Arrive at the Powell Library located at the University of California, Los Angeles campus no later than 10 p.m. Park in the library lot found on Charles E. Young Drive. When you arrive, find Ari Schneider." Yes, this is all of the information I received. Imagine my surprise when I arrived at an enormous cocktail party that had been underway for several hours. After locating a fellow caterer, I discovered that work for the party began at 12 p.m. The first shift was working until 10 p.m, when the second shift was set to arrive. The swing shift would finish serving guests, clean-up, and then breakdown. After everything was finished, I crawled into bed at 7 a.m.

As one can imagine, the entire episode was so hectic, it took thirty minutes to find Ari Schneider. After I found the short, angry, bald man, he said, "Make yourself useful and find something to do." Not the best advice for a new employee who has never been trained by the company.

Although the job offered an inconsistent work schedule, I remained a loyal member of this clandestine enterprise. During peak summer season, the company scheduled numerous catering shifts throughout the week. In the winter months, parties and events were more infrequent. The November before graduation, I picked up a side hustle for a small Internet startup. This story could have been more incredible if this company became Instagram, Venmo, or Twitter. Instead, this little tech company created quirky software for a small niche in the field of higher education.

On the second day of work, the boss said, "We know you're a minister, but just so you know, both of your supervisors in the office are gay. Is that going to be a problem?"

I locked eyes with David, my new employer. "No, that's not going to be a problem, but it might become a problem next year when I graduate seminary and begin a self-righteous career judging other people from the pulpit. Until then, I'm still learning the proper techniques of alienating others."

After drilling an uncomfortable laser beam into my soul, uncontrollable laughter filled the small office space. This brief exchange began our journey as coworkers, friends, and eventually confidants.

No one would describe the job as exciting or challenging. However, the work hours were flexible. Most days, I sat quietly in the office doing data entry and organizing office equipment. A month after being hired, David stopped hiding his feelings about Christianity, his parents, and church.

"I've hated the church since I was seventeen years old. One morning I was a beloved son getting ready for school, the next I was living on the streets of Hollywood struggling to survive. My life began spiraling out of control after I told my parents I was gay. Without saying a word, my father marched into my bedroom, stuffed my belongings into a trash bag, and pushed me out the front door. As I stood sobbing in the cold, my mother handed me a crumpled-up wad of bills. Not even a high school graduate, and I was given less than fifty dollars to start a new life; a life where my parents could hide their gay son."

With few alternatives, David left the Los Angeles suburbs and moved to Hollywood. At seventeen years old, he did not have the necessary skills to financially support himself, so he began working as a male prostitute. By the age of nineteen, he contracted HIV. By twenty-one, he was a full-blown drug addict sleeping on the streets in Santa Monica. Imagine for a moment how different his life would have been if his family would have embraced his sexual orientation.

David was in his early fifties when we became friends. At this stage in life, he was entering his twentieth year of sobriety, his deepest friendships were formed at his local Alcoholics Anonymous group, and he hated church. As we were locking up the office one night, our relationship began to evolve.

"Andy, I don't hate God, but I sometimes question why God would make me this way. I've endured so much pain and hardship because I am physically attracted to men."

With great trepidation, I asked, "Do you think God made you this way?"

With the polarizing question hanging in the air, David fired back. "I certainly didn't choose to be this way! Why would I choose to be gay and be disowned by my family? I was forced to live on the streets at seventeen years old. Andy, no one wants to believe their baby will grow up to be a drug addict living on the streets. I was discarded by my family after coming out of the closet. My parents forced an uneducated teenager onto the streets. Turning twenty-dollar tricks was how I survived. No one should have to endure this pain. I would never wish that lifestyle on my worst enemy." With tears filling his eyes, David continued, "Andy, this is how I was made. It's so hurtful when people think that I chose this lifestyle."

I understood why David felt ostracized by his family's church. His childhood was filled with Sunday School, vacation Bible School and youth retreats. Sunday mornings were sacred until he came out as gay. I found his story heartbreaking. He was disowned by his family, rejected by his friends, and cast aside by his local Christian community.

David exemplifies the men and women Jesus encounters throughout the Gospels. Jesus fervently sought to build relationships with the lame, crippled, blind and disgraced outcasts who were forced to live outside the gates of the city. These children of God struggled to survive in the margins of society. Their days were spent begging for food, water, and the kindness of strangers just to survive. David was not physically or mentally handicapped. He was not a danger to his community. He was a sweet, compassionate child of God who had been mistreated, abused and discarded by his Christian community. Jesus, the son of God, would never have treated David, or any person, in this manner.

In Mark 10:46-52, readers first encounter blind Bartimaeus, a man so disgraced he was simply known as the son of Timaeus. Think about that. This poor man was not even worthy of a formal first name. One afternoon, the blind man was sitting outside the gates of Jericho. A few moments later, he would encounter Jesus, and it would change his life forever. As the rustle of footsteps drew closer, the blind man cried out, "Jesus, Son of David, have mercy on me!" The crowd demanded that the blind man be quiet, but he knew this was his opportunity to be restored; a chance to return to the living. With great faith, he yelled again, "Son of David, have mercy on me!"

Jesus heard the blind man's cries for healing. With great compassion, he told his followers, "Call him here."

Seizing the opportunity, the disciples summoned the blind man, "Take courage, stand up! Jesus is calling for you."

Without hesitation, the blind man tossed his beloved cloak onto the ground, rose to his feet and came into the presence of the Son of God.

As he drew closer, Jesus asked, "What do you want Me to do for you?"

The blind man responded, "Teacher, I want to regain my sight!"

Jesus responded, "Go; your faith has made you well."

Immediately, the son of Timaeus regained his sight and became a follower of Jesus.

When the blind man encountered the Son of God, he knew exactly what he wanted. He asked to be healed from blindness. Blind Bartimaeus went for it all. Full vision returned him to full standing in his community.

During the six months I worked with David, I did not respond as he expected. I did not read him Scripture or pray for his wayward soul. Instead, we hung out as friends, and I asked questions about his life. A few times, we went dancing together at nightclubs in West Hollywood, an area often referred to as Boy's Town. I met his best friend, who happened to be a part-time drag queen. We shared long walks after work together. I wanted to know David as a person. I wanted to understand his struggles and be a part of his pain. We became friends. We went out to dinner. We had lunch. We would call each other on the phone. We would talk about our favorite movies. I would tell him what I was learning in seminary. However—and this is the key—I never tried to change David, only understand him.

David did not need healing from his sexuality identity. He needed restoration. He needed to be loved, accepted and recognized for the man he was created to be. Jesus, the Son of the Most-High God, desired for his beloved to return to full standing with his family and community.

During adolescence, everyone within my sphere of influence believed people chose to be gay, lesbian or transgender. Our pastors and youth leaders discounted biology and scientific data. More than once, the men stepping up to the pulpit would proclaim that homosexuality is an abomination to God. In this narrow viewpoint, members of the gay and lesbian community are going to be banished to the depths of hell. These destructive messages create painful separations. As a result, it's easy to understand why people who identify with the LGBTQ community distance themselves from the Christian faith.

The church is not always going to get it right. As a matter of fact, the church is going to continue to be an institution that causes unintentional pain and suffering. Until the pews grow more and more empty on Sunday mornings, the church will continue to create painful emotional scars.

On my final day of work after my six-month partnership ended, David gave me a hug and said, "I just want you to know that for the first time in over thirty years, I'm open to the idea of Jesus because it's the first time I felt somebody from the church wasn't judging me for being gay." Then he said, "Thank you, Andy."

DATING DISASTER

In my early 20s, I could be best described as a dating disaster. I had no idea how to talk to women. I had no idea that women didn't want to have long discussions about youth ministry, professional sports or my current workout plan. I had no idea how to dress or style my hair. Do men even style their hair? I was often left asking the question, "What's wrong with me? Why don't women like me? I'm a nice guy. I stay in shape. I have a stable job. I have nice parents. I have all my teeth. My body odor seems normal. So, what's wrong with me?"

It wasn't until I met my future wife, Dodi, in the second year of seminary that I learned nothing was wrong with me. I just needed extra time to develop the necessary skills to be a committed partner. When we first met, it was anything but fireworks. Our initial interaction was more like a porcupine trying to hug a grizzly bear.

We were introduced by friends who thought we would be perfect for each other, because we both like to pump iron. After sharing our innermost gym secrets, Dodi asked to borrow my truck so she could move apartments. Now, being the gentleman that I am, I said, "Absolutely, you can borrow my truck. Matter of fact, I'll fill it up with gas and throw in a free air freshener."

The next morning, I arrive at her apartment at ten sharp and toss her the keys. With a twinkle in my eyes, I say, "Here you go. I can grab my truck later today after I hit the gym."

Dodi must have been stunned by my supreme generosity. Because she responded, "I thought you were going to help me move."

"You didn't ask me to help you move. You asked to borrow my truck. I don't want to spend my entire Saturday moving boxes and furniture."

She stared at me for a long moment. "Yeah, moving sucks. That's why you have friends to help."

Obviously, I wanted to be a man of my word, so I explained, "You didn't ask me to help you move. You asked to borrow my truck, and I planned on a long workout at the gym, but I hope to catch you later."

For all the single people in the world, this not a solid first impression. Even worse, this beautiful woman would soon become my wife and mother of our two children. Thankfully, Dodi forgave my ignorance and rudeness, and a year later, we went on our first date. We walked from her apartment to this little pizza place in Pasadena. On our way to grab frozen yogurt for dessert, I noticed a cashew in the middle of the busy street.

Being the consummate gentleman, I asked. "Would you like

that?" Much to everyone's surprise, she said no. So, I picked it up and ate it. The moment that dirty nut touched my lips, we burst into uncontrollable laughter. It was one of those glorious laughs when your stomach aches and you struggle to catch your breath.

With a little spring in our step, we hustled over to the frozen yogurt place. As we spooned frozen deliciousness into our mouths, we swapped inappropriate youth ministry stories and laughed until our eyes began to water. At the end of the night, I walked her back to her apartment, gave her a long hug and promised to call for a second date. Being the clueless idiot that I am, I didn't call her. Why? There's no reason.

One afternoon, I run into her on our small campus. She saunters over and says, "I thought we had a good time. Why didn't you call?"

Surprised and impressed by her confidence, I managed to say, "We did have a good time, and I would love to see you again." Thank goodness for smart empowered women. Without Dodi's self-assurance, I am not sure how our story would have played out. Fortunately, she was able to break through all of my personal walls of protection and careless shortcomings. She is truly a woman who makes me want to be a better man.

CHAPTER 12

HOLLYWOOD SQUARES

"Comedy comes from a place of hurt. Charlie Chaplin was starving and broke in London, and that's where he got his character 'the tramp' from. It's a bad situation that he transformed into a comedic one."—Chris Tucker

WHAT DO YOU DO FOR A LIVING?

It was six years after bombing at Chris Tucker's Comedy Club in Atlanta before I finally gained the courage to move to Los Angeles. Despite my long-term ambitions to become a minister, it was time to face my comedy fears. With little guidance, I began scouring the Internet for a comedy class to serve as a springboard stand-up on the West Coast. Less than a mile from my apartment, The Ice House Comedy Club was offering a ten-week stand-up comedy workshop. The class was taught by Los Angeles-based comedian Bobby Oliver, who has been teaching Comedy Workshops for aspiring comedians for over twenty years. The workshop offers students from diverse backgrounds a safe and supportive platform to practice the art of comedy. Class alumni continue working in the entertainment industry as writers, actors and comedians.

After completing Oliver's ten-week course, students are given the opportunity to perform a graduation show on the Ice House main stage. Without hesitating, I raised my hand to perform. Five months after relocating to the entertainment capital of the world, I was again facing my fear of failure. To prepare for the show, I spent countless hours memorizing, fine-tuning and rehearsing a five-minute routine. During the initial stages of stand-up, delivering a funny five-minute routine feels like an eternity. At four minutes, the red light in the back of the room flashes to offer a one-minute warning. A comedian who ignores the warning lights is subject to a verbal beatdown from the club manager and show's producer.

Word of my upcoming performance quickly spread across the small seminary campus. On the night of the show, twenty classmates came out to support me. Standing in the green room, I offered a short prayer, "God, I do not want to be rich or famous, but please do not let me bomb on stage." With all the strength I could muster, I proudly walked on stage to grab the microphone. My opening line that night, "Before we begin, I want to take a moment to thank my hair product for making my hair look so good tonight." That stupid little joke worked. The audience laughed, and we were off and rolling, which was great because it is key for the audience to laugh at your first joke. Over those next five minutes, I invited the audience to laugh about my learning disabilities, depression and abstinence.

The strangers in the audience found it difficult to believe I was studying to be a minister. An exuberant woman yelled out, "If you're really a minister, I'm ready to confess my sins." Her outburst shook my rhythm, but I collected my thoughts and said, "It might be hard to believe I'm going to be a minister, but remember this, someone has to be the worst one." This off-script comment captured the attention of the audience. In this awkward moment of laughter, I was able to transition back into the well-rehearsed routine. "People outside the church are often concerned about my celibacy. Please, don't worry about my celibacy—because it's not premarital sex if I'm not planning to get married." After this punchline, the rest of the evening was a blur. But as I climbed into my bunkbed that night, I knew I was hungry for more time onstage.

HOW CAN YOU HELP?

In Los Angeles, people love to ask, "So, what do you do for a living?" I soon discovered that what people were really asking is, "What can you do to help my career?" People seeking to climb the ladder of success will naturally gravitate toward individuals who are ascending on an upward trajectory. With limited comedy experience in Atlanta, it was impossible to understand the cutthroat nature of the entertainment industry. When fellow comics in Los Angeles discovered I was a struggling seminary student, I was discarded with yesterday's trash.

Everything came tumbling down one Friday night while performing at the world-famous Comedy Store located on the Sunset Strip. I was scheduled to open the show for a host of up-and-coming comics, including nationally recognized comic Don Friesen. When the show's promoter discovered none of my friends came to support the show, I was dropped from the scheduled lineup.

Four hours later, I was given three pitiful minutes of stage time. As I walked through the curtains, an eerie silence had filled the desolate theater. Squinting into the lights, I saw that only one person was left in the entire theater—an older gentleman waiting to lock up for the night. Instead of making the poor guy suffer, I picked up the microphone and asked, "You need help locking up?" Thirty minutes and three trash bags later, we locked the front doors and headed home.

The experience was soul-crushing. I thought the show's promoter was my friend, but we weren't friends; I was just a glorified ticket broker trying to sell seats for his show. The moment I became a financial burden, my allotted stage time was given to the next eager comedian willing to fill seats with paying customers. Comics who attract paying customers are desirable commodities.

As a point of reference, ministers who attract large donations are highly sought-after commodities as well. Far too often, an individual's value is determined by financial success. By American standards, Jesus's ministry would have been considered a failure. Senior Pastor, the honorable Reverend Jesus Christ, would have endured a short reign as mega-church leader. Our Lord and Savior would have been promptly replaced with a charismatic speaker offering feel-good sermons.

I AM NOT A CHRISTIAN COMIC

This is not meant to be offensive, but I am not a Christian Comedian. I do not tell jokes about growing up in church, reading the Bible, or the countless hours I spend in prayer. It has never been my desire to perform comedy for strictly Christian audiences. It has always been my desire to offer clean comedy which succeeds outside the confines of the Christian community. Both Christians and non-Christians can identify with my struggles as a minister, father and husband. I refuse to use Christianity as a crutch to gain stage time.

For those who question my moral compass, just remember I am a Christian who happens to perform stand-up comedy. What's the difference? I do not pander to the Christian community. My comedy is free from vulgarity, sexual innuendo, and political commentary, but it is not written strictly for Christian audiences.

No one asks my wife if she is a Christian business owner.

She is a Christian who owns a business. My father was a mortgage broker for over twenty-five years, but he was not a Christian mortgage broker. Former NFL Quarterback Kurt Warner is a devout Christian, but no one calls him a Christian quarterback. He is a devout follower of Christ who has been blessed with a million-dollar arm. Thanks to Warner's status as a Super Bowl Champion, he has been afforded numerous opportunities to share his Christian faith.

I have never been shy about my Christian faith, and I am always willing to engage in a healthy dose of self-deprecating spiritual humor. More than once, I have been asked why I became a minister and often reply, "It's obviously for the exorcisms. Casting out demons is an untapped market." Some people become offended when I make a comparison between boiling a lobster and baptizing an infant. Come on! It's a joke, people. I would never put rubber bands on a child's hands before submerging him into the baptismal fount.

CHRISTIAN SHOWS

After getting my feet wet in California, I was constantly searching for stage time. I have performed at innumerable crummy bars, coffee shops, and fundraisers for a pitiful ten dollars in gas money. Needless to say, if a church with an eager audience was willing to pay more than gas money, I eagerly waved my hand to take the gig. Money pays the bills, but comedy provides a unique opportunity to cleanse the soul. As such, stand-up is not always financially lucrative, which creates the need to love the struggle.

After a year of hustling gigs, I was thrilled to be invited by several well-known Christian comics to serve as the opener for a large show in Orange County. After receiving the invitation, I knew this was only the beginning of my successful career as a clean comic. The sanctuary was packed with over fifteen hundred audience members. This was my moment to shine. I boldly walked onto the stage and unloaded a twenty-minute routine about a stolen truck, our neighborhood crack dealer, and missionary work with heathens living in Canada. I received a great round of applause after finishing my set. In my mind, I was amazing.

Riding on the proverbial Cloud Nine, I was mentally preparing for our next show together. After the show, however, everything came tumbling down. Feelings of promise began rising as the promoter walked over. He gently placed a hand on my shoulder and said, "Sorry, Andy, we're not gonna use you anymore."

"What?" I thought, "I just nailed it!" At least I thought so.

After the show, a local pastor unloaded on the show's promoter because I shared a story about a former girlfriend that he deemed to be inappropriate. Reverend Conservative was furious because I offered a fabricated tale about my father, who is the master of the worst-case scenario.

The Genesis for this ridiculous story took place during seminary when I was dating a young woman my family didn't like. I remember telling my father about the relationship, and he responded, "Oh, no, son. Oh, no." Naturally, I was concerned about why my dad was so upset. Without hesitation, he said, "You shouldn't be dating her. She's going to end up pregnant."

I was shocked by his response and reassured him, "No one is going to get pregnant, Dad."

"Son, next thing you know, you're about to become a father. You're not finished with school. You don't have a full-time job. You don't have enough money to pay the bills. She's going to leave, and there you'll be, left to raise a baby all alone. Next, you and the baby will move into your childhood bedroom. You will drop out of school and work two full-time jobs. And here I'll be —a seventy-year-old man left raising a one-year-old baby. No, son. I do not think you should be dating this woman."

It was a joke. The whole idea was meant to serve as a ludicrous scenario. The conservatives in the audience became upset when I challenged a real-life scenario. Heaven forbid the church should talk about real issues. People do have sex before marriage. Sometimes babies are born out of wedlock. Grandparents might step in to help a struggling parent. This stuff happens. We should be talking about it. We should be willing to laugh about it. Instead, I was cast aside as an inappropriate Christian comedian.

I DON'T EVEN WANT TO BE KNOWN AS A CLEAN COMIC

In an effort to make a name for myself, I avoided the labels "Christian Comedian" or "Family Friendly Comedy." Despite the content of my material, I do not want to be pigeonholed by assigned labels. My performances are free from swear words, potty humor, and crude sexual humor. However, being labeled a clean comic can serve as slow toxic stage death. Just ask Sinbad. However, I have zero interest in gravitating toward shock value to generate laughter. Like most comedians, the stage is more than a platform to make people laugh. The stage, microphone, and audience creates space to humorously explore children, career, marriage, childhood and friendship.

Over the years, people have said, "Oh, you should do more jokes about being a minister." Despite the encouragement, jokes about being a minister are too personal. As a result, audiences do not know how to appropriately respond. Sometimes it's fun to make the audience uncomfortable, but ultimately, comics are trying to entertain. As a stand-up, you're standing in the spotlight armed with only a microphone to protect yourself. You are often inviting the audience to laugh at the darkest and most painful moments of your life. Every moment, your insecure inner voice is crying out, "Please love this joke."

Don't get me wrong, I have tried to poke fun at my career as a minister. But I can witness people become visibly uncomfortable when I say, "You know what, our little church leadership team believes I am already overpaid. As a result, they decided not to give me a Christmas bonus this past year. Can you believe that? The church decided not to be generous on Christmas. Being the good minister that I am, I rewarded myself with a handsome bonus from the collection plate on Christmas Eve. This might sound wrong or even criminal, but we should be placing the blame on the stingy leadership team."

This outlandish joke makes Christians, Muslims, wizards, and warlocks uncomfortable. Even the local atheist becomes upset when the minister jokes about dipping into the church offering. The entire scenario is meant to be ridiculous, but audiences are uncomfortable laughing at inappropriate jokes from the local clergy. No one really thinks I am scooping quarters out of the offering plate to wash my clothes at the local laundromat. In these moments, it reminds us how closely we guard spirituality.

HOW TO SUCCEED IN THE WORLD OF COMEDY

To succeed in the harsh world of comedy, stand-up comics must embrace the unpredictable patterns of victory and defeat. The euphoric highs are amazing, but the emotional lows are worse. Every bomb feels like a personal attack, and every failure feels like the universe is threatening your career. Being paid to make people laugh is not an easy job. Performing stand-up comedy is an extended exercise in vulnerability. Anyone can repeat funny jokes into a microphone, but not everyone is a gifted performer. Becoming a successful comedian takes perseverance, failure, and resolve.

It is imperative to love the struggle if you are going to survive in the cutthroat world of entertainment. Stories of overnight success are one in a million. Every setback must serve as a learning opportunity. An affinity for Cup-o-Soup and 99-cent menu items is a must. Cramming into a crummy, two-bedroom apartment with four roommates becomes the best way to save money. For perspective, I slept in bunkbeds with my twenty-seven-year-old roommate. While we were sleeping soundly in our bunks, a struggling musician was asleep on our bedroom floor.

Before embarking on a comedy career, please understand your education will be earned on stage. No amount of practice or writing can prepare individuals for the thrill of entertaining an audience. Every great comedian has paid their dues performing free shows for undeserving audiences. Rhythm and timing can only be developed through years of practice. It is easy to make people laugh off-stage, but everything changes when you step into the spotlight and see an audience staring at you, poker-faced, expecting to be entertained. Your best friend laughs at your silly stories because you're both rolling with the ebb and flow of the conversation, and because he or she understands you and your personal history. However, you are a stranger to an audience. They have no emotional connection to you, and they are not searching the stage for a new friend. They come seeking the healing power of laughter to reduce the stress of their lives.

WHAT HAPPENED?!

Three years after relocating to California, it was time to make difficult decisions. Pursue a career in ministry or take the path less traveled and become a full-time comedian. Becoming an established, working comedian requires full-time dedication to the craft. A true performer will never excel if they are only willing to dip their toes into the pool. Whether you sink or swim, a career in comedy requires a cannonball into the deep end. The same can be said for many jobs. It is difficult to have a full-time impact when you are only receiving part-time pay for part-time effort.

For musicians, comedians, and especially magicians, the key for long-term success is finding the best way to change the audience instead of constantly trying to create a new show. Remember, a joke is inherently funnier the first time you hear the punch line. An upstart Jerry Seinfeld did not perform the same routine every weekend at the same venue. Instead, he hit the road searching for different audiences to fine-tune his material. As a result, aspiring comics pay their dues by spending at least half the year performing shows on the road.

Here is a brief snapshot of what a week on the road might look like. A Saturday-night performance at Topeka's TopCity Comedy Club finishes with a cramped motel room on the outskirts of town. The Sunday morning routine becomes two generic energy drinks, a banana, and a pack of crackers. After devouring the healthy breakfast, it's time to make the five-hour drive to Oklahoma City for a five-night gig at the Loony Bin Comedy Club. A week later, the three-hour drive to Dallas looms on the horizon. The Lone Star is uncharted territory, always searching for new performers to fill their clubs, bars and theaters. After exhausting the time of local comedians and promoters, it's time to hop back into the car and head to the new comedy festival in New Orleans.

For up-and-coming comics, long, crazy weeks on the road become the new normal. To establish longevity, comedy must serve as your raison d'être; making people laugh must become the core of your being. As performers claw their way to the top, they must avoid comparing themselves to their peers. This idiom should be true for every passion in life. We cannot let our lives be dictated by what society deems to be the traditional path to success. A life full of passion should serve as the measuring stick for success.

CHAPTER 13

ARE YOU SO READY?

"How do I move the Atlasphere? Well, I use anything I can. I'll use my legs, my hands, anything I can find to make the thing move. Oh, and if a contender is in the way, I can slam them out of the way, too."—
Thunder, an American Gladiator

NOT MAROON 5

On the first night of filming, Adam Levin, not to be confused with the lead singer of Maroon Five, tore his anterior cruciate ligament in a game of Power Ball. Minutes after assessing the severity of the injury, NBC called.

"Andy, one of your fellow contenders was hurt during filming. You have been selected as the first alternate and will need to be here for competition at eight a.m."

"Wait. What? Adam got hurt? Is he okay?"

"Andy, Adam will be okay, but he needs to be replaced in the competition. You have been selected to take his spot. If you're not here at eight a.m., you will not be given another chance to compete."

I HATE COFFEE

After exiting wardrobe and make-up at 8:30 in the morning, I was placed in the holding room. There was nothing to do except read textbooks for class. There was no television, Internet, or music—just a blank room with a couple of granola bars and water.

At nine a.m. sharp, a burly man burst through the doors. "Are you ready? Are you *so* ready? Andy, you don't look ready! You're going on stage in less than an hour! You need to be ready!"

Every thirty minutes, he would burst through the door and say the same thing. "Are you ready? Are you *so* ready?" And every time, I would reply in a mellow voice, "Yes, I'm *so* ready."

He was not pleased with my reserved demeanor.

"I appreciate your willingness to get me hyped-up, but I'll be ready at go-time. You don't need to worry about me."

Excess caffeine and nervous energy had the veins in his forehead firing on all cylinders. "Andy, you're going on in thirty minutes! Now, put that book down and get ready!"

As anyone else would respond, "I'm ready, but I would like to finish this chapter. I'm in the middle of final exams, and I really need to study. I have a C in Church History at the moment, but if I get an A on the final exam, I can move my grade to a B."

It became clear that I was not going to derail his hype train. "You're going on in less than thirty minutes! You need to be ready!"

Glancing over from the boring pages of church history, I said, "Don't worry. I'll be ready. When I walk onto the floor, I'll flip the switch and be ready to compete. So, don't worry—I am *so* ready."

After fueling up on church history and yogurt-covered raisins, it was finally time to compete. My first event would be the Joust, where I would square off with a behemoth of a man who called himself Titan.

To begin, gladiators and contenders were strapped into harnesses then hoisted onto a twenty-foot platform by a crane. After exiting onto the platform, competitors and gladiators were given giant Q-tips to do battle with. Titan was loaded with 250 pounds of solid muscle. Yes, the whole scene was meant to be intimating.

The audience was filled with family, friends, and my future wife, Dodi. With all eyes set on center stage, the announcer shouted, "Gladiator, are you ready?"

Titan hollered, "Ready!"

"Competitor, are you ready?"

With slight trepidation, I calmly responded with a nod.

"Ready! One, two, three . . . go!"

Within a split second, we were smacking each other with our pugil sticks. With one strong blow, I caught Titan off-balance. He wobbled.

"Oh, my gosh," I thought, "I am going to win the Joust!"

I had hardly finished the thought when he landed a counter-strike, and I was free-falling into the freezing cold water below.

Flopping around like a house cat in a bathtub, I struggled to the ladder where Laila Ali was waiting to ask questions.

"Andy, what happened?"

These types of questions never receive great answers. To anyone watching, it was obvious that I simply lost. Bobbed when I should have weaved. Zigged when I should have zagged. One moment I was tasting victory, the next I was taking the swim of shame.

To add insult to injury, Titan yelled from his victorious platform, "What happened to you, Frodo?"

Yes, I was heckled on national television by a gentleman who outweighs me by several hundred pounds. Trying to cut him down to size, I responded, "Hey, Titan, I love your fake tan!"

MOVING TO THE SEMIFINALS

In each episode, competing contenders would participate in events against the gladiators. The goal—earn as many points as you can battling the gladiators before tackling the final obstacle, The Eliminator. Each event was given an assigned point value. The gladiators were determined to keep competitors from scoring points. In the Joust, for example, competitors could earn ten points for winning. Each point separating the contenders would translate into a half-second lead at the beginning of The Eliminator.

Before running The Eliminator, my fellow competitor, high school teacher Sharaud Moore, was carrying a ten-point lead. His lead gave him a five-second head start. Until our episode, four minutes was the fastest Eliminator time.

On the first whistle, Moore scaled the eight-foot wall and jumped into the pool. Five seconds later, I was slashing through the water hoping to pass him. Pulling myself out of the water, I noticed he was falling behind. I scaled the cargo net, cranked through the hand bike, ascended the pyramid, soared down the zip line, and struggled to complete the reverse travelator.

Bursting through the finish, I completed The Eliminator in a little under two and a half minutes. The crowd went wild. Thoughts of winning the show began to flood my mind.

"I am going to win *American Gladiators*! I'm going to be invited back next season to compete as *a* Gladiator! I'm going to be an American freakin' Gladiator. I'll call myself the Saint! It's my big break! I'm going to be famous!"

A few hours later, my dreams were crushed by Evan Dollard, who finished The Eliminator in less than a minute and a half, more than a minute faster than my time, without even breaking a sweat. Despite his amazing performance and the sinking feeling in my stomach, though, I moved on to the semi-finals to compete against Alex Rai.

SEMI-FINALS

Hit-and-Run was the first featured event in the episode titled *Preacher vs. Teacher.* During the events, competitors ran between scoring platforms on a wobbly bridge. While running, gladiators were swinging giant weighted balls at the competitors' heads. As I returned to the scoring platform, one of the hundred-pound medicine balls smacked into my temple. Losing all sense of balance, I toppled from the bridge into the water. I struggled to the edge of the pool, scoring only two points. At the end of the first event, Rai was carrying a 6-2 lead.

During our second event, Hang Tough, contenders were given sixty seconds to traverse a suspended platform using multiple sets of hanging gymnastic rings. On the opposite side of the scoring platform stood the gladiators, waiting for a chance to pull competitors into the water. A maximum of ten points could be earned in the event.

Instead of taking home ten points, I managed to play keep-away from the gladiator known as Justice, thus scoring five points. Alex was caught by Justice and scored zero points. This victory gave me a one-point lead heading into the third event.

Next came the Joust. Both competitors were forced to do battle with The Wolf. After losing against Titan the first time, I was ready for a chance to redeem myself. For this round, I set my feet in a traditional snowboard stance and swung my padded stick with as much force as I could muster. Much to everyone's astonishment, I knocked the gladiator into the water. My response was, "Wow, that even surprised me." Looking to save face, The Wolf launched into a vicious assault against Alex. Rai didn't last too long on the platform, and my lead grew another ten points, 17-6.

The fourth event was The Gauntlet. Each contender was given the opportunity to be thrashed in a padded half-pipe by four massive gladiators brandishing unforgiving blocking pads.

In the 2008 NBC revival of the show, each contender had to avoid all four gladiators and crash through the finish blocks to receive a full ten points. If a contender failed to complete the entire course, two points were awarded for completing each section being guarded by a gladiator.

With only a few seconds remaining on the clock, I was able to slip past the final gladiator to earn ten points. When his turn came, Alex launched onto the course, determined to earn ten points, but just a few feet from crossing the finish line, Toa knocked Rai to the ground with a vicious shoulder to the chest. Thanks to this valiant effort, he was awarded six points.

Moving into the final event before The Eliminator, I was carrying a 15-point lead. Alex was a fierce competitor. I needed every point to give myself a chance to move on to the final round against Evan Dollard.

The last event was The Wall, a 40-foot rock climbing wall with a scoring platform on top. Contestants raced up the wall while being chased by the gladiators. Upon reaching the top, the winner would receive ten points, while the contestant in second place could earn five points if they avoided being pulled into the water below.

Seconds before reaching the top of the wall, I lost my balance on one of the climbing holds. This slight mishap created the perfect window for Alex to slip past. It was a photo-finish at the top, but Alex hit the button first. He was awarded ten points, and I received five points for avoiding the gladiator.

It was almost time for The Eliminator, and I was carrying a ten-point lead, or a five-second head start. On the first whistle, I launched into the course full of determination. I was determined to hold my five-second lead and finish the course ahead of Rai. I charged through the water onto the cargo net. My lungs were already on fire by the time I reached the hand-bike. I looked over and saw Alex gaining ground. I raced up the pyramid and down the zip line to the final obstacle known as

The Travelator. Twenty more feet, and I would be competing in front of millions of fans to be crowned as the next American Gladiator. I didn't care about the money; I wanted a chance to crush fellow contestants.

I clawed to the top of the reverse treadmill; victory was in my grasp. Mere seconds before victory, I stumbled into a downward backslide to the bottom of the Eliminator. It was not a spiritual backslide, just a painful failure witnessed by millions of people. It's no big deal; no one remembers the misplayed ball to lose the championship game.

Lying at the bottom of the obstacle in a sweaty pile of spandex, Rai came zooming past. The crowd was going wild, and the noise was deafening. Everything seemed to slow down, and my focus landed on Rai and his assault on The Travelator. On his second attempt, he cleared this brutal obstacle with ease. Full of heartbreak, I watched my fellow competitor burst through the finish line.

The loss was devasting. I had nothing left. I spent every ounce of physical and emotional energy. I had the lead, with victory in sight, and I lost. From my perspective, I was not defeated by my competitor. I lost. Alex Rai was an amazing competitor and a gracious victor, but losing was still hard. I had the lead for the majority of the competition and only lost in the last few seconds. For almost a year, I had recurring nightmares about stumbling only moments from victory. Ten years later, the loss still hurts.

PICKING UP THE PIECES

Months after the show aired, friends and strangers discussed the loss. Instead of allowing the wound to heal, outsiders continued to pick the scab. On a weekly basis, I would receive emails, phone calls and text messages saying, "I can't believe you lost."

Friends would ask what happened. I always felt like yelling, "I lost. I freaking lost! It is one of the most painful moments in my life; one I would love to forget." With claws raised, I wanted to ask, "Is there a painful moment you want to discuss?"

I was blessed with fifteen minutes of fame, but becoming a C-list celebrity on *American Gladiators* altered the trajectory of my life. Appearing on national television gives strangers an open invitation to critique your life. People at the gym said, "If you trained harder, you would have won." I became a target on social media. Numerous times, outsiders attacked or belittled my Christian faith. Yes, I chose to compete, but I sometimes wish I never had to talk about the experience.

Anytime we lose something, the results can be devastating. However, perseverance in the face of adversity will strengthen our resolve. It teaches us to get back up and continue fighting. We may not succeed today, but we will never achieve victory if we quit.

Competing on *American Gladiators* is not the end of the story, nor is it the beginning of the journey. Instead, it is just one of the beautiful moments that shaped my life. Today, it serves as a small snippet of the story I've struggled through in life. Every setback, failure and disappointment carries the ability to serve as an amazing opportunity for growth. Muscles cannot grow without exercise. In turn, our spiritual and emotional muscles must face adversity to grow. A phoenix needs a powerful fire before it can rise from the ashes.

CHAPTER 14

FRESH WOUNDS

"The more I get to know Jesus, the more trouble he seems to get me into."—Shane Claiborne

THE AMERICAN GLADIATOR LOSER GRADUATES SEMINARY

. . .

Two weeks after millions of Americans watched me compete and lose on American Gladiators, and two months before graduating Fuller Seminary, I obliterated my right knee. On a Friday morning in early March, my roommates and I made the 90-minute drive from our apartment in Pasadena to Mountain High Ski Resort. We had planned to hit the terrain parks for a couple of hours in the morning and then hustle back for a comedy gig later that night. Our standard routine began with warm-up laps on the mountain's smaller terrain parks. After we built enough courage or located a backpack full of stupidity, we would head over to the advanced terrain park to hit the big jumps.

Around lunchtime, it was time to challenge the 40-foot booter at the beginning of the big terrain park. This particular jump would launch riders 50 feet through the air, more than the length of a school bus. Full of false bravado, I thought, "No problem. I got this." At the highest point of the jump, daredevil seminary students and fearless teenagers soar 20 feet off the ground. Proper speed is imperative for landing these larger jumps. If you hit the jump with too much speed, you overshoot the landing. If you don't hit the jump with enough speed, the snow will jump up and smack you in the face. Milliseconds before launching myself into the air, I knew I didn't have enough speed. Soaring off the ground, I kept thinking, "I'm not going to make it. I'm not going to make it. Oh, this is going to hurt. This is going to hurt really bad. This is going to be awful." In a desperate effort of self-preservation, I begin to flap my arms like a duck. If I can just roll the windows up fast enough, maybe I can gain the few extra feet of airtime to clear the jump.

Nope, I crashed directly into the unforgiving snowpack. On impact, the entire weight of my body slammed onto my right knee. There was an audible snap of a tendon, like a shotgun being fired into my ear. Boom! The sound reverberated throughout my body; it was the total annihilation of my patellar tendon. The same patellar tendon that had been serving as my anterior cruciate ligament for the past ten years.

The doctor who repaired my ACL when I was 19 years old said, "You will never tear this patellar tendon graft. It will be as strong as a steel cable." Full of ego, he added, "Matter of fact, if you tear it again, I will give you a full refund." Yeah, right.

Despite the doctor's prior assurance, the steel cable became string cheese. The violent impact ripped the inside of my right knee to shreds. The pain was unspeakable. Sprawled across the bottom of the jump, there was no question I had been seriously injured. With too much pride, I refused to call ski patrol for help. With all the strength I could muster, I limped my fragile ego and injured knee down the mountain.

Hours later, I crawled onto the top bunk of shame. As I

looked up at the blank desolate ceiling, fear and failure again became the dominant themes. In the next couple of months, I would need two, possibly three surgeries to repair my broken body. In addition to the freshly torn anterior cruciate ligament, the labrum in my right shoulder had been torn while I competed on American Gladiators. As if these current injuries weren't enough, I was dealing with the pain from a torn rotator cuff in my left shoulder. This injury occurred during a college rugby game, but I had been putting surgery on hold. However, the pain in both shoulders was no longer manageable.

After the snowboard accident, I was a physical, emotional, and spiritual wreck. In less than two months, I would graduate seminary, and I had zero job prospects on the horizon. Friends and classmates started to finalize their plans after graduation. Most had jobs lined up. Several were making wedding plans, and many were relocating to new cities. This was not the outcome I had expected after three years of seminary and standup comedy. I erroneously believed I would be a hot little commodity in the Christian world.

Hot commodity, not so much. The financial burden had started to grow. With very little money in my checking account, I was facing a series of expensive surgeries. Followed by months of intense physical therapy. I could no longer work for the catering company because of the knee injury. I didn't have a side hustle to support my limited income. Despite the throngs of resumes and applications I submitted to churches across the country, one church, just one church, pursued me for their open youth pastor position.

TOP OF THE WORLD

Just a few months earlier, I opened a comedy show for Kenn Kington in Fresno, California. I walked onto stage and was greeted by 2,000 people who were hellbent on having a great time. After the show, Ken casually handed me an envelope, "Andy, great set tonight. Thanks for making the drive up. I hope to see you in the near future." Once inside my truck, I opened the envelope and was surprised by a check for $1,500. I had just been paid $1,500 to make people laugh for twenty minutes. Yes, standup comedy was definitely going to be my calling.

In addition to being a working comedian, I fulfilled a childhood dream by competing on American Gladiators. People within my circle of influence insisted my television appearance would just be the first of many. As the surreal experience began to take root, I told myself, "Andy, this is your big break. This is the moment you have worked so hard for. Your comedy career is going to soar to new heights after the show airs. This is just the beginning."

Based on the outcome of the first episode of American Gladiators, random churches, strangers, and former coworkers were coming out of the woodwork to express their support. Instead of staying grounded, I let fifteen minutes of fame go straight to my head. Through a shallow viewpoint, I falsely believed the exposure on national television would launch a lucrative comedy and speaking career. I envisioned churches across the country offering top dollar to hear my real-life David versus Goliath story.

Yet, just one church, located in Jacksonville, Florida, extended a job offer. The church sent a Facebook message, "Andy, everyone in our congregation rooted for you on American Gladiators. We were impressed by your character, poise, and faith. We firmly believe God is calling you to be our next youth pastor. Under your leadership and guidance, our youth group will flourish. We will reach more kids for Christ than ever before. In closing, our hiring committee would love to set up an interview to discuss your transition to Jacksonville."

After reading the email, I started an Internet rabbit trail to learn more about the church and the city of Jacksonville. The church appeared to be a healthy and vibrant congregation governed by conservative Christian values. According to numerous websites, Jacksonville is a great place to live. It has a nice selection of restaurants, sporting events, and outdoor activities, but it was not a place I wanted to live after seminary. As a result, I politely told the church, "No, thank you." A couple of days later, I received another message from the hiring committee. "Andy, we just know God has called you to be our next youth pastor."

With little hesitation, I replied, "Thank you for the generous job offer. I am flattered by your interest, but we are not a match at this time. Please let me know if I can help identify potential job candidates for your organization."

This determined church refused to take no for an answer. As a follow-up, the church tracked down my friend and mentor, Chris Reny. At the church's request, Chris called to help expedite the interview process. "Andy, if this church wants you this bad, you should give them a chance. There is no harm interviewing for this job. From what I'm hearing, you don't have numerous churches knocking down your door with job offers. You don't need to take the job, but you owe it to yourself to set up an interview."

"Chris, I don't want to move to Jacksonville. That's not where I want to be."

"Just give them a chance, man. You could love it. By the way, I sent your number to the hiring committee."

The church wasted no time making personal contact. For their initial phone call, they recruited an eighty-year-old grandmother whose soul was spraying bolts of spiritual humility. "Andy, I had a vision that you were anointed by God . . ." (Yes, anointed by God.) " . . . to be our next youth pastor. God has called you to serve the youth of our church. Under your leadership, these young men and women will encounter the glory of Jesus."

In seminary, we were never taught about receiving a personal anointment from God. As a matter of fact, I was uncertain if an unsuspecting individual can be anointed. For reference sake, I have never been able to baptize or marry an individual without their knowledge or consent. Sure, Jesus, the son of God, was anointed, but we're talking about Jesus. LeBron James, one of the greatest basketball players of all time, has been anointed by the basketball gods, but we're talking about King James.

At the end of the phone call, I told the sweet grandmother that I would like to interview for the position with her church. To prepare for the upcoming hour-long phone interview, I created a list of twenty questions I might be asked by the hiring committee. However, anticipating the upcoming interview questions was not enough. Next, I began to form answers for the questions I had created. From my limited perspective, I concluded that the answers needed to be clear, succinct and theologically sound.

Answering the interview committee's questions was step one. To complete step two, I had to form a list of specific questions I wanted to ask. Step three was to assure the church that I was the best candidate for the position they were looking to fill.

Despite all of the interview preparation, I managed to study for the wrong final exam. The hiring committee did not ask any of the questions I was prepared to answer. They could have lobbed a few softballs to hit. Well that didn't happen. Nope they went rogue with the first question, "Andy, why do you want this job?"

For over two years, I studied improv comedy at Improv Olympics in Hollywood. Despite years of being asked to bark on command, my improv techniques were nowhere to be found during this interview process. *Curse you, improv comedy lessons!* I thought. *These people are looking for answers, not potty humor.*

Caught off guard by the initial question, I uttered a weak

response. "Well, I am flattered by your continued interest. For close to a month, various church members have refused to take no for answer. Based on your persistent nature, I thought scheduling an interview was appropriate."

My unenthusiastic answer created an emotional vortex that sucked all of the life out of the interview. At this point, we should have punched the time clock and called it a day. Instead of yanking the emergency brake, the committee trudged forward with their questions. "Andy, based on your initial response, do you even want this job?"

"At the moment, I am not sure. I thought this phone interview was an opportunity to assess one another. It's possible we are a great fit. On the other hand, we might decide I am not the best candidate for the job."

For another painful sixty minutes, we pushed through a series of bizarre questions for which I had limited answers. Here is one example, "Andy, what is one luxury item you cannot live without?" Or how about this one, "If two students are competing in different sports on the same night, which sporting event will you attend?"

Any minute, I was expecting someone to ask, "Andy, if one train leaves Topeka, Kansas, traveling at 120 miles per hour, and another train leave Carson City, Nevada, traveling at 70 miles an hour, which train will be the first to reach Salt Lake City?" (For curious parties, the train from Carson City should arrive first.)

PASTOR SHEETS AT BEDSIDE BAPTIST

For five straight weeks, this church from Jacksonville, Florida chased me like a golden retriever playing fetch. One pitiful phone interview later, I heard nothing, not even a follow-up email a week later. Two weeks after the interview, I called the head of the hiring committee.

"Hi. This is Andy Konigsmark in Pasadena, and I'm calling about the status of my application for the opening for the youth pastor position." The secretary says, "Let me put you on hold for a moment." She gets back on the phone and says, "Oh, I'm sorry, Mr. Konigsmark. We don't have an answer yet, but I'll have a member of the hiring committee call you back once your application has been reviewed." I hung up thinking, "Once my application has been reviewed? According to everything I had heard, this was my job if I wanted it."

A few more weeks went by, and crickets. I scrolled through my phone log to contact the sweet grandmother who made the initial phone call. "Hey, this is Andy Konigsmark at Fuller Seminary. I was calling to check the status of my job application."

"Can you say your name again? What is it?"

"Andy Konigsmark."

"Let me check my records here. No, I'm not seeing your name. When did you interview for this position?"

Totally shocked, I said, "Remember, you said I had been anointed for this position when we first spoke on the phone. I thought I would hear back in a couple of days about the status of my application."

With all the sweetness she could muster, she said, "Well, I am sorry to inform you that the church has decided to move forward in the hiring process. At this time, you are no longer being considered for this position. I am certain God has bigger things in store."

I hung up the phone and was left dumbfounded. In my arrogance, I thought I was a lock for this job I didn't want. It wasn't my best interview, but dang, I had been discarded like yesterday's trash. As I was collecting my thoughts inside the dumpster, I came to the realization that it was one month from graduation. I needed to move out of my apartment, sell my bunkbed, and find a job, yet I hadn't been offered a job by a single church, ministry organization, or fast food franchise.

Full of despair, I begin littering different churches, non-profits, and mission organizations across the globe. I planned to send at least twenty resumes or letters of interest every day for a month straight, which would equate to some level of contact with at least 600 different organizations.

IT'S THE END OF THE MONTH

By the end of the month, I was no longer being particular about the jobs I applied for. Yes, this type of job search can be considered desperate. Just remember, it's always easier to find a job when you have a job. People can smell fear in your resume.

Fear became the motivating factor in my job search. I was experiencing a deep sense of loss and helplessness. This tumultuous experience at the end of seminary was stirring up all of the negative feelings I had experienced after moving back to Montana for graduate school. I felt completely broken and helpless.

How had I reached this point again? I made good grades. I made contacts. I tried to broaden my circle of influence. It seemed like everybody was getting jobs except for me. My roommates were moving out, but I was living in an empty apartment. Within a couple of days, I would have to shoulder the responsibility of paying the bills previously shared by four people.

In the midst of my bi-annual downward spiral, a close friend called. "Andy, there is a job opening for a part-time youth pastor in Aspen, Colorado. I think you should apply for it."

I wasn't certain I could afford Aspen as a full-time minister, let alone as a part-time youth minister. Yet, the job description and desirable location had captured my attention. The position became more appealing when I discovered the salary package included free housing. Armed with enough information to make a foolish decision, I contacted the senior pastor to set up an initial interview.

In the first informal interview, the pastor asked numerous questions tailored toward my specific skill set. The first question: "How do you feel about relocating to a small town with a ski problem?" Great, next question please. "What do you enjoy about working with youth?" Their energy and passion; plus, their ability to laugh at themselves. Being around middle and high school students presents the perfect opportunity to slow down and enjoy life. "What will be your greatest strength coming to this community?" Without question, it will be my ability to identify with the outdoor culture. Mountain biking, rock climbing, and snowboarding fuel my soul. As a result, I will have numerous opportunities to blend my growing faith with my passion for the outdoors.

Less than a month later, it was time for an in-person interview. The time had come to impress the judges with immense theological knowledge. I hopped a redeye from LAX to Denver; then drove four hours to Aspen to begin the formal interview process. Shortly after I arrived at the church, the interview was set to begin. Before I was able to make myself comfortable, a member of the interview committee said, "I looked up your name on the Internet. " Everyone is caught off guard as the room fills with uncomfortable silence. With complete control of the room, she asked "Why didn't you tell us about competing on American Gladiators? " My answer, "I didn't think it was relevant. It's just not one of those things that comes up organically in conversation. It would have been awkward to say, looking forward to meeting everyone on Friday. By the way, I was on American Gladiators."

I received a phone call from the church two weeks after the in-person interview to officially offer the position. Initially, the job was going to be part-time, with housing. To support myself, I needed to secure another part-time job within the small community. Members of the church asked, "Andy, what are you going to do for work?"

"I'm recovering from two shoulder injuries, but when I am fully healthy, I'll return to the service industry as a bartender or server." The service industry had been my bread and butter for close to fifteen years. It has never been my passion, but it offers flexible hours with solid pay.

A few of the older church members were concerned, "Ooh, I don't know how we feel about you being a bartender. It would seem to make more sense to be a substitute teacher. Being at the school would present the best opportunity to meet students outside of church."

No child dreams of being a bartender or a substitute teacher, but both professions are in demand. However, a substitute makes maybe $120 on a good day. Plus, you have to deal with kids who make it their mission to make life miserable from the moment they discover their regular teacher is out sick or skipping school. I'd rather make $50 a day scrubbing toilets than be humiliated by a group of eighth-graders. Needless to say, I have been a part-time bartender, part-time minister, and full-time disappointment to my seminary professors for the past eleven years.

CHAPTER 15

FIRST CALL

"I was raised around heterosexuals, as all heterosexuals are. That's where us gay people come from—you heterosexuals."—Ellen DeGeneres

SOMEBODY LET THIS GUY BECOME A MINISTER

Despite my good-natured intentions, strangers are caught off-guard when they learn I am an ordained minister. They are not upset about the baptisms, sermons or outdated hymns. Instead, I become a magnet for individuals who loathe the Christian faith. Their religious experience has filled them with anger, frustration and disappointment. A negative church experience during early adolescence has created life-defining tension for millions of American adults. For many, the church no longer serves as an agent of change. For critics, the Christian Church represents everything wrong with religion.

During a mountain bike ride last summer, a friend asked, "Do you believe in science?"

With as much sarcasm as I could muster, I answered, "Science is the work of the devil. From the beginning of time, scientists have been trying to destroy the majesty of God. Scientists claim the earth was created by the Big Bang. No, I don't believe in science."

As I finished spewing these ignorant though satirical words, we began cranking up a steep climb. Our chests were heaving with fury when we reached the top of the hill. After finally catching our breath, my friend said, "I really enjoyed your line about science being the work of the devil."

For the record, I do not believe science is the work of the devil. Nor do I believe, however, that every answer can be found within Scripture. For example, the Bible never mentions the complexities of organizing a fall wedding during college football season. Conversely, science and technology are unable to answer which restaurant cooks the best pulled-pork sandwich in Georgia.

This may come as a surprise, but there is no mandatory statement of faith for Christians. Regardless, far too many churches insist that their congregations must profess the same opinions, values and beliefs. Instead of accepting our beautiful differences, Christians of all denominations enforce theological boundaries. These boundaries create walls of division rather than houses of worship.

Jesus never instructed his followers to construct rigid dogma. Instead, the Son of God told his followers, "Love the Lord your God with all your heart and with all your soul and with all your mind. This is the great and first commandment. And a second is like it: You shall love your neighbor as yourself. (Matthew 22:37-39)." Jesus's message throughout the New Testament is inclusive, not exclusive. Instead of focusing on the transformative love of Jesus the Christ, our churches cling to and bicker about doctrinal differences.

ARE YOU CALLING ME EVANGELICAL?

In our small ski town, the words Christian and evangelical have become interchangeable. For many, the word evangelical is synonymous with the religious right, the Christian political movement characterized by strong, socially conservative values. These conservatives, including fundamentalist Christians, remain vehemently opposed to the science of evolution, abortion, and same-sex marriage.

An interesting footnote: a growing percentage of fundamental Christians are demanding that our government protect gun rights. The New Testament does not provide a relationship between guns and Jesus, but I've certainly heard Christians declare that gun ownership is a God-given right.

For people standing on the sidelines, evangelicals represent everything wrong with religion, church, and Jesus. News outlets typically portray evangelical Christians as anti-gay, anti-science, and pro-life.

Mainstream media and politicians have hijacked the word *evangelical.* Even the beloved preacher, Billy Graham, a prominent leader in the conservative Christian movement, found difficulty defining the term. His response was, "Actually, that's a question I'd like to ask somebody." The English word *evangelical* originates from the Greek word *euangelion,* meaning "good news." The good news is that Jesus, the son of God, broke into this world to suffer with humans. This good news was consecrated with the life, love and compassion of Jesus as his spirit conquered death. Through the grace of God, the spirit of Christ dwells in our hearts. If we are able to remove the political connotations, this is certainly great news.

GUMMY BEAR

After officiating a friend's wedding ceremony, my wife and I stayed for dinner to celebrate. Upon being seated, one of the guests offered our table some cannabis-infused gummy bears. Recreational marijuana became legal in Colorado in 2012. We said thank you for the offer and politely declined the gummy bears. At first, I did not give our decision a second thought. In the past, friends and acquaintances have offered a friendly toke on the chairlift. Sharing the pipe is synonymous with ski resort culture. When offered, I've always said, "No, thank you." No harm, no foul. No bad feelings. No judgment. We move on to the next run and quietly rip down the mountain.

This time was different. After declining the gummy bear, a young lady at our table began unloading her negative feelings about religion and Christianity.

"Are you one of those evangelicals who thinks you're better than the rest of us because we're getting high? Maybe you're just going to sit here silently judging us."

My eyes grew large, and my ears became hot with embarrassment. Mustering a quiet sense of resolve, I responded, "I feel it would be poor form for the minister to get high at the wedding and then drive home to meet the babysitter and kids."

The keyword in this phrase was "feel." It is difficult for feelings to be wrong.

She did not like my feelings and turned course to launch into a new attack. "I'm pro-choice, and I hate the Republican party. How does that make you feel? Do you think I am an evil person because I support abortion?"

In less than a minute, we had leaped from gummy bears to abortion. The conversation was rapidly moving downhill. I was surprised by the outburst, so I took a few moments to collect my thoughts. Weddings are a time to celebrate, not an opportunity to discuss religion or politics. This young lady must have been carrying a host of negative feelings toward religion and Christianity.

As a minister and representative of Jesus, I must temper negative thoughts and impulsive overreactions. I said, "I am sorry if I have offended you, but we're here to celebrate. If I am ruining your dinner experience, we can move to another table."

Much to my chagrin, the guest was unwilling to accept the apology. At this point, we politely excused ourselves from dinner and drove home. Here's the point—Christians and non-Christians must be willing to admit fault. Forgiveness is essential to navigating life's difficult journey. Spiritual and emotional health require a spirit of forgiveness to thrive. Therefore, we must embrace our world with a humble spirit.

GUNS AND JESUS

While delivering a sermon before the upcoming 2012 presidential election, a church member asked, "Andy, who should we vote for in the upcoming election?"

As a faithful leader, I responded, "You must vote for the person who best represents your values."

This answer did not satisfy the congregation. Another church member asked, "Who are *you* going to vote for?"

At this point, I should have used evasive maneuvers. To my detriment, however, I replied, "Over the years, I have voted for both Republicans and Democrats. As I said, you must vote for the person who best represents your values." This benign response upset the majority of our politically conservative congregation.

After service, I joined a church member for lunch to discuss the sermon. A verbal assault began before our food arrived. This older gentleman started attacking my unspoken politics. He could not believe I would ever vote for a political party that allowed women to murder children. Next, he challenged American gun laws. He could not believe I would support a president who wanted to take away his guns. I argued that I never said I wanted to take away his guns; I said we must vote for the candidate who best represents our values. I have never told church members I am pro-choice, anti-gun, or a member of a certain political party. As a minister, you are tasked to walk a tightrope of social justice. Every word and action must point toward God's eternal love, irresistible grace, and unmatched mercy.

GAY SKI WEEK

In 1977, Aspen's Gay Ski Week roots were first planted. The early years consisted of informal house parties and hot tub get-togethers. By 2013, the small house party became a week filled with special events. The Aspen community embraces the week-long festival with food, cocktails, and spontaneous drag shows. Guests from around the globe come to ski, dance, and mingle. In recent years, the Aids Fashion Show has become the highlight of the week. In partnership with the Telluride AIDS Benefit, $2.7 million dollars has been raised to support local and global organizations who continue the fight HIV and AIDS.

Rainbow flags are hung all over town to celebrate the week-long festival. Storefronts post signs which read "Welcome Gay Ski Week." A local gas station hangs a large banner, "Make America Gay Again." In February of 2016, in response to the festivities, I changed the church sign to read *Welcome Gay Ski Week*. Within minutes of creating the new sign, I received numerous phone calls from the leadership team and disgruntled church members. Everyone was asking the same question: "Why did you put that on the sign?"

The sign was not intended to be controversial. On the contrary, it was intended to diffuse some of the negative tension between Christians and members of the LGBTQ community. After receiving numerous phone calls asking that the sign be removed, I asked the dangerous question, "Are people who attend Gay Ski Week not welcome at our church?"

The answer was emphatic. "Of course, they're welcome, but our church does not need to be so bold." I felt that if our churches remain shrinking violets when it comes to difficult issues, outsiders will remain on the outside. If we believe Jesus is the Risen Christ, we should throw open our doors to invite everyone to the banquet. In Luke 14:21-23, Jesus proclaims, "Go out at once into the streets and lanes of the city and bring in here the poor and crippled and blind and lame." And the slave he was speaking to replied, "Master, what you commanded has been done, and still there is room." Jesus said to the slave, "Go out into the highways and along the hedges, and compel them to come in, so that my house may be filled."

There is no hint of exclusion in Jesus's words. Instead, he boldly proclaims that everyone is welcome at His table. At the Divine banquet, we will encounter Democrats, Republicans, socialists, gays, lesbians, blue collar workers, chief executive officers, immigrants, the just and unjust. Every creed, race and color are welcome. Jesus cannot be impressed by clothes, money or power. For our churches to further the kingdom of heaven, we must let the offensive words of Jesus penetrate our hearts.

A growing percentage of the LGBTQ community find themselves being persecuted by the evangelical Christian community. This public persecution excludes God's Children from Jesus's banquet table. Our little Colorado church must confront injustice. Outsiders should walk past American churches and know they are welcome.

After calling an emergency leadership team meeting, two hours were spent debating the pros and cons of our *Welcome Gay Ski Week* sign. Removing the sign would send the wrong message. One suggestion was changing the sign to read *All Sinners Welcome* because keeping the sign welcoming gays might upset some conservative church members. Again, however,

Jesus was never concerned about upsetting people within his community. Lest we forget, Jesus became angry and started flipping tables in the temple. People were not happy with his actions.

The welcome sign added for Gay Ski Week was not the first time I placed a welcome sign for the community. Before the start of the community's annual Film Festival, I placed a sign which read *Come to church and avoid the long movie lines.* At the beginning of the 2011 NFL season, our church sign asked, *Does Jesus love Tebow or Tom Brady?* A few months later, I ran an ad in the local newspaper stating, "Tired of that cold chairlift? We have a warm seat for you on Sunday morning."

But the ad that made me lose my sign and newspaper privileges was, "Upset about the Denver Broncos' first round pick? Let's pray about it."

I did not support the *All Sinners Welcome* sign because current scientific data suggests 2-3 percent of our population is born with a same-sex attraction. Consequently, many individuals who identify as gay, lesbian, bisexual, or transgender do not consider their lifestyle a sin. We are all sinful from birth, but our sexual orientation should not be considered a sin if we want to offer a safe environment for the LGBTQ to worship God.

In Jesus's day, physical disabilities such as blindness or leprosy were attributed to the sins of the parents or the individual. In John 9:1-3, Jesus responds to his disciples about this misaligned belief system. "As (Jesus) passed by, he saw a man blind from birth. And his disciples asked him, "Rabbi, who sinned, this man or his parents, that he was born blind? Jesus answered, "It was not that this man sins, or his parents, but that the works of God might be displayed in him."

The blind man, whom modern readers encounter in John 9, was cut off from the world because of physical limitations. In first century Jewish culture, Temple leaders forbid individuals with severe physical disabilities to worship in the House of God.

As a result, the religious leaders forced the outcasts to live on the margins of society. Subsequently, the untouchables who lived outside the city gates were labeled unclean.

Yet Jesus refused to describe anyone as unclean. His earthly mission sought to eradicate the barriers which kept outsiders from God's love and restoration. He proclaimed to the crowds that restoration of sight brought glory to God. With new-found vision, the once visually impaired man became an equal member in the community. Members of the LGBTQ community do need healing from their sexual orientation; for theirs is the Kingdom of Heaven. In response, Christians must call upon Jesus's mercy to heal our spiritual blindness.

The Samaritan people were another group who were ostracized from Jewish society. The Jews were taught from birth to hate the Samaritans. However, in John 4:7-9, Jesus stands contrary to the religious expulsion of the Samaritan people. A woman from Samaria came to draw water. Jesus said to her, "Give me a drink." (For his disciples had gone away into the city to buy food.) The Samaritan woman said to him, "How is it that you, a Jew, ask for a drink from me, a woman of Samaria?" (For Jews have no dealings with Samaritans.) A Jewish man asking for a drink of water astonished the Samaritan woman. Jesus did not see a Samaritan woman. He saw a woman whose life could be transformed by the love of God. Remember, being born a Samaritan is no more a sin than being born gay or lesbian.

Unfortunately, many in the American church have unconsciously agreed to treat members of the LGBTQ community as Samaritans. In Luke 10, Jesus shares the passage of the Good Samaritan. To paraphrase, a local Baptist minister and an Episcopal priest see an older man, who has been beaten badly, laying in a filthy ditch. The man desperately needs help, but the priest and minister cross the road to avoid him. A short time later, a young gay man who has been rejected by his family and church, scoops the badly injured man into his arms. This modern-day Good Samaritan carries the badly-wounded man to the local hospital to receive medical treatment. He offers to pay all of his medical bills and promises to check on him. Jesus shares this story to shatter our expectations. We want to believe our Christian leaders will lead the way, but it is the young gay man who shatters our perfect image of church.

MARRIAGE

As a conservative Christian teenager, I erroneously believed God created wholesome marriages with gummy bears, cotton candy rainbows, and fountains of Mountain Dew Code Red. These magical relationships filled with loads of glitter and smiles would be nourished through copious amounts of sex. As a devoted husband, I've come to learn healthy marriages involve difficult conversations, professional conflict, and personal struggles. To remain emotionally connected, partners must provide tremendous compassion, immense benevolence, and unlimited forgiveness. Marriage is hard work for couples of every creed, color, and orientation. Life doesn't provide a magic formula to create marital bliss. As a result, all marriages are subject to a series of trials and tribulations.

Our first year of marriage was a recipe for disaster. I'd already moved to Colorado when I proposed to Dodi. Regrettably, she was living her best life in Southern California when I slid Aunt Carl's diamond ring on her finger. Moving to Colorado meant leaving an amazing group of friends, a steady paycheck, and long weekends at the beach. She was willing to move, but her newlywed dreams never included an expensive ski town in the middle of the Rocky Mountains. Her dreams always involve sunshine, beach towels, and flip-flops. Instead, I promised huge snowstorms, arctic mornings, and frozen windshields.

The second mistake, we became pregnant approximately twenty minutes after walking down the aisle. Maybe not twenty minutes, but Dodi was pregnant six weeks after the honeymoon. We did everything in our power not to conceive a child. However, we learned an important lesson the first month of marriage; sex works. Even when you don't know what you're doing, it still works.

The third mistake, our little church in Colorado promised free housing. Yes, the housing was free but completely unstable the first year of marriage. In a twelve-month period, we needed to move four times. Less than two weeks before Emmi Claire was born, a nasty property manager gave us forty-eight hours to find a new place to live. Six weeks after her birth, we moved a fourth and final time. While all of this was taking place, I was desperately searching for my rhythm as a part-time minister, part-time busboy, and full-time husband. I don't know much about marriage, but I know it's hard.

MARRIAGE IS HARD

Six years after accepting the position as part-time youth pastor, I remained on staff at our sweet little Baptist Church. Southern Baptist Missionaries founded our sweet little church in 1982. The first installed pastor created a statement of faith which continues to guide the theologically conservative congregation. The original statement includes several doctrinal statements which appear archaic and out of date. A God-centered marriage can only exist between one man and one woman. Members of the congregation must oppose all forms of sexual immorality, including adultery, pornography and homosexuality. Women were not allowed to have authority or leadership over men. Finally, the pastoral team must abstain from all forms of debauchery. Really, all forms of debauchery?

The winds of change shifted in October 2014, when same-sex marriage became legally recognized in Colorado. Ministers and churches across the country realized it would only be a matter of time before their biblical interpretation of marriage would be challenged by federal law. Less than a year later, the U.S. Supreme Court would legalize same-sex marriage in all fifty states. Change was coming, and many Christians were unprepared to respond.

Even before seminary, I was conflicted about same sex marriage. I've always believed the LGBTQ community is beautifully and wonderfully made. Our family believes God loves everyone. Church should be a home of inclusion, rather than an instrument of exclusion. But many of us received a different message from our religious leaders on Sunday morning: same-sex relationships were an abomination to God. In Genesis, we find the first marriage taking place between one man and one woman. As a result, Christians, and especially their clergy, should not condone marriage between same-sex partners.

LET'S GET MARRIED

On a brisk January morning in 2014, my cell phone began to ring moments before I exited the chairlift to snowboard down the mountain. A woman called to ask if I could perform a wedding for her daughter, Beth. This mother had been referred by a close friend who insisted I perform the ceremony for her daughter. These phone calls are routine for a young minister living in a resort town. During a normal year, I perform over twenty destination weddings for couples looking to get married in the scenic Sangre de Cristo Range.

For those who are uncertain, I am not an Elvis impersonator working at a Vegas wedding chapel. This means short-notice ceremonies are not my specialty. As a faithful minister of word and sacrament, one script does not fit every situation. Call me old fashioned, but I believe wedding ceremonies are sacred moments. For marriages to prevail, individuals must cling to one another for better, for worse, for richer, for poorer, and remain steadfast in sickness and health. Lest we forget, a wedding ceremony is a commitment to the future more than the present. Faithful couples vow to build a future together. This commitment involves more than exchanging rings. For marriages to endure the trials of life, vows must serve as timeless guidelines to shape the future.

Considering the sacred nature of weddings, couples and wedding planners book my services at least six months in advance. Colorado is an interesting state with regard to marriage. Within the confines of the Centennial State, couples do not need an officiant or minister to be married. They can walk to the courthouse at noon, sign the paperwork, and be legally married fifteen minutes later. A marriage license does not require a blood test, background check, or forty-yard dash time. Nope, Colorado makes marriage easy.

When the bride's mother called, I was focused on charging down the slopes for at least an hour before a midday work meeting. It is all about priorities, people. Originally, Beth and her fiancé were planning a fall wedding in Virginia. However, the beauty of the Rocky Mountains changed their plans. If possible, they wanted to be married in a Christian ceremony before returning home.

After deciding which black run to tackle first, I checked my calendar and informed Beth's mother I was free to perform a short ceremony the following morning.

"Thank you so much, Andy. My daughter and her partner will meet you in front of the courthouse at ten a.m."

In a rush to get off the chairlift, I didn't ask the fiancé's name or what the couple was planning to wear for the ceremony. When I arrived at the courthouse, the young couple perceived a look of surprise on my face.

"Will this be your first time marrying two women?"

I replied, "A couple of years ago, I asked my wife if we could have a sister wife. She wasn't interested in sharing her closet with another woman."

Sensing apprehension, Rachael, the fiancée, introduced herself and began sharing her story. She had been raised in a conservative Christian home where homosexuality was considered an unforgiveable sin. During high school, she buried her same-sex attractions and tried to date boys, but no amount of prayer or reading the Bible could change her same-sex attraction. She hid her sexual identity until she graduated from college. After landing her first job, she built up the courage to tell her parents she was in love with another woman. Her family refused to listen. After just one conversation, Rachael became an outcast.

Her parents refused to embrace a daughter who lived in defiance to God. Their conservative faith would not allow them to embrace the possibility of same-sex attraction. No amount of science or biology could reconcile an all-loving God allowing their daughter to love another woman. Rachael told her family she had noticed an attraction to girls since grade school. Boys did not pique her interest. Her parents, siblings and relatives refused to listen. A gay daughter was not welcome in their family.

At this point, Beth's father chimed in, "If Rachael's parents will not accept this beautiful woman as their daughter, then I will become the proud father of two girls."

Beth looked at me for a moment, "Are you going to marry us?"

With little time for personal or theological reflection, I said, "After hearing that heartbreaking story, of course I'm going to marry you."

The thought of joining two women in marriage makes many fundamental Christians furious, but rejecting these women on their wedding day was not the proper response. If Beth and

Rachael were rejected by a Christian minister on their wedding day, they would never feel welcome at church. Over the years, these young women have received absurd amounts of oppression from members of the Christian faith. Instead of focusing on the sexuality of others, Christians should focus on establishing the love of God here on earth. This perfect love encompasses the entire world. Jesus may not have joined two women in marriage, but I am certain the Son of God would have offered them a seat at his banquet table.

Being anti-gay is far easier when nobody in your inner circle is a member of the LGBTQ community. However, things begin to unravel when your son introduces the family to his high school boyfriend. Picketing the local Planned Parenthood Clinic is considered acceptable until your daughter admits to paying for an abortion. Lest we forget, no one goes to the abortion clinic on the best day of their life.

Despite the words of Jesus, there are very few churches in America denying church membership, leadership roles, or volunteer opportunities because of the sin of divorce. Thousands of divorced pastors lead their congregations every Sunday. At present, the church is quick to forgive divorce, infidelity and spousal abuse.

However, a large percentage of churches continue to alienate members of the LGBTQ community by labeling their lives as sinful. No one wants to be judged or called sinful. As a result, our gay and lesbian friends do not feel welcome in the house of God. Jesus never intended for his teachings to be exclusive.

To break this destructive cycle, the church must engage in more compassion than criticism. Christians must be people of inclusion, rather than exclusion. Church is not an elite country club where members are forced to pay their dues. No, the church is meant to be like grandma's dinner table. Everyone is welcome at grandma's house as long as you wipe your feet and remove your hat.

CHAPTER 16

I'VE WORKED HERE FOR TEN YEARS

"If anything is good for pounding humility into you permanently, it's the restaurant business."—Anthony Bourdain

IT'S A DARK INDUSTRY

Please don't act surprised when I tell you the American restaurant culture is filled with alcohol, drugs, and impulsive decisions. As dinner service ends, the late-night party begins with legal and illegal substances. Loyal customers do not realize the constant barrage of substance abuse that destroys romantic relationships, exacerbates mental health issues and often leads unsuspecting individuals down a variety of destructive paths. Unless you work at Chick-fil-A, heavy drinking and frequent drug use is the accepted culture.

Wide-eyed and full of ignorance, I began a well-paid career as a bartender and poker dealer as a twenty-one-year-old college student. There are many challenges associated with late nights and cash tips. Not a single teacher, professor or religious leader thought to mention the potential challenges. For those who are unaware, America's food service industry ranks number one for illicit drug use and alcohol abuse. Throughout the years, I've witnessed countless restaurant employees battle the demons of substance abuse. One rowdy night, the waitstaff witnessed a disastrous Batman impersonation. Filled with a strong dose of stupidity and liquid courage, a co-worker climbed the tallest building in Gotham City. With a full head of steam, he sprinted towards the edge of the roof. At the last possible moment, he propelled his body into the darkness. I am certain, his intoxicated state of mind created false bravado. To no one's surprise, our friend did not have the juice to clear the ten-foot gap between rooftops. Instead of floating through the air like a sugar glider, he tumbled from the roof and wedged his crumpled body between two air conditioner units. Within minutes of the accident, search and rescue scaled the building to save our critically injured co-worker. His legs and ego were broken in the accident, but he was not fired for this act of stupidity (and people claim there are no more miracles).

WHAT WAS YOUR DREAM?

"Dad, when you were a little boy, was it your dream to work at a restaurant?" asked our eight-year-son on a recent road trip. Embarrassed by the question, I told my little boy that I originally wanted to grow up to be a golden retriever. When my canine dreams were crushed by my kindergarten teacher, I decided to become a professional baseball player. Except there was a small problem with my Big-League dreams: I was cut from the high school team before tryouts even began. The coach pulled me aside, "Son, you aren't going to make the team. Instead, you should focus on an easy sport, like soccer." When my soccer career fizzled out my freshman year of college, I embraced a call to ministry.

Yes, I followed the call into ministry, but after eleven years, I remain on part-time salary. Our sweet little church would love to support two full-time ministers, but this dream has yet to become a reality. As a result, I continue to hustle for part-time shifts at the restaurant to support our family.

On the best days, I embrace the duality of being a part-time minister and bartender. The polarizing professions create freedom and generate an endless supply of comedy. These opposing occupations often produce organic opportunities to address the spiritual and emotional needs of the local community.

On the worst nights after the bars close, I drive home feeling like a full-time disappointment. I criticize myself for not securing a full-time job to support my wife and kids. I complain about the hustle. I become frustrated with Christians who believe my lifestyle is progressive, post-modern and relevant. Paying the mortgage on time is relevant. Knowing all of the ingredients in a Long Island Iced Tea is just part of the job.

UNACCEPTABLE

One particular incident at the restaurant provides the perfect summary of life after graduating from Seminary. It was a snowy night in the middle of ski season when a ten-person party arrived in our private dining room for dinner. Within a few minutes of sitting down, an expensive bottle of wine was being poured for the table. Appetizers, steaks, and sides had been ordered. Everything was moving along according to plan. It was a typical restaurant experience, until it wasn't. When it was time for the entrees to arrive, only half of the steaks made it to the table. Somewhat baffled by the lack of food, I hustled into the kitchen to check with our executive chef. His response was pretty clear, "You only ordered five steaks, with zero sides."

A bit incredulous, I asked, "Why would I only order five

steaks for a ten-person table?" The chef was not too happy with the question, but it turned out the kitchen only received half of my order. We discovered later that there was a problem with the printer. For some reason, only half of the ticket printed. If we had caught the mistake earlier, we could have avoided the problem.

At that point, there weren't too many solutions to immediately rectify the situation. The table could either wait patiently for their steaks to be grilled or they could cancel the order. Armed with an answer, I headed back to the dining room and explained the situation to the head of the party. Immediately, the father became upset. He pressed his foot on the gas pedal and began shouting, "This is unacceptable! Unacceptable! This is unacceptable!"

The situation had gone from bad to worse. It was apparent that I would not be receiving a strong Google review. I looked the father in the eyes and said, "Sir, I am really sorry. What can I do to make this situation right?"

The father considered the question for a moment and said, "There's nothing you can do. This is unacceptable. You have ruined my vacation."

Wow, the meal went from unacceptable to a ruined vacation. The father demanded I clear the prepared food sitting on the table and return when the entire meal was ready. This might sound simple, but our restaurant is a high-volume establishment with an undersized kitchen. There is very little wiggle room for mistakes; steaks are only grilled after they are ordered. This should be a simple concept to understand, but a steak cannot be cooked faster. For guests to receive their food on time, orders must be right the first time.

As one can imagine, the father did not care to hear our kitchen's unique design flaw. My explanation, too, was "unacceptable."

I told the father the truth. "Our kitchen is working on the

steaks. Everything should be ready for the table in about fifteen minutes. When your bill comes, we will buy a few items to express our sympathy."

Undeterred, the father commanded the attention of everyone within earshot. "We will never eat at this restaurant again. Your service is unacceptable."

Fifteen agonizing minutes later, the entire meal arrived at the table. After the father took his first bite, I asked about the quality of his New York strip. With wine dribbling down his chin, he responded, "This is the best steak I have ever put in my mouth, but your service is unacceptable."

Despite the father's immense displeasure, he devoured his twenty-ounce steak in a matter of seconds. As I poured his third glass of wine, I asked, "Sir, is there anything we can do to make your experience better?"

Guzzling his wine, he replied, "Young man, there is nothing you can do to make this situation right. Nothing."

At the end of dinner, our general manager came over to apologize for the confusion. To no one's surprise, the father took this moment to express his extreme displeasure with the service his family had received. Much to his dismay, he forced himself to admit the quality of the food was excellent. However, he went on to say that the restaurant's service was unacceptable and had ruined his family's last night of vacation. Our GM chose the high road by purchasing the family's entire meal. With wine, appetizers, and dessert, the total bill was about $1500. Yes, you read that correctly. I paid $1100 for my first car. I presented the father with an empty check, explaining that our general manager graciously covered the entire bill. I told him we did not want anyone to leave our restaurant disappointed. Upon receiving a free meal, most people would say thank you, but the disgruntled father refused to accept our generosity. His immediate reply was, "You will not buy our meal."

At this point, I was completely lost and befuddled.

"Sir, I'm very sorry," I said, "but my general manager does not want you to leave the restaurant with any negative feelings. I am sorry for the inconvenience. I feel we have done everything within our power to resolve this unfortunate situation."

The father was unwilling to let it go. Something inside his DNA would not allow him to receive our generosity. He barked the word unacceptable one more time before leaving the restaurant—without paying. His final, parting shot was, "Here's a piece of advice—maybe it's time you quit working as a bartender."

The father didn't even leave a tip on a free meal. Twenty percent of their original bill would have been three hundred dollars, yet he chose to leave nothing. I am fully dependent on the generosity of customers and church members to support our young family. Yet, he was not interested in the financial needs of a young father. Waiting an extra fifteen minutes for steaks was a reprehensible, unpardonable sin.

On Sunday morning, I rubbed the sleep out of my eyes and walked behind the pulpit, ready to deliver the sermon when out of the corner of my eye, I noticed the family from the previous night's dinner. In that moment, I changed the beginning of my sermon. "As many of you know, I work at a local restaurant as a bartender to support my family. I had never considered this until recently, but as a minister and bartender, our family is fully dependent on your generosity. When people withhold generosity, it directly affects my family; it creates stress and discord. Your generosity has allowed my family to purchase a home, save for college, and hopefully retire one day. I cannot say this enough, but this community has faithfully provided. Thank you."

At this point, I made eye contact with the father. "Please remember, generosity opens your heart. Withholding generosity can cripple your soul. When you withhold tips from your server, you might be punishing a father who is dependent on tips to support his family. I feel that financially punishing your server or bartender is *unacceptable* in the eyes of the Lord. If we are withholding a twenty-dollar bill from the poor father who is slaving away to take care of his children, I hate to think about what we might be withholding from God.

"From my point of view, your generosity pays for groceries, preschool, and dance lessons. As Christians, we should be the most compassionate and kind-hearted people in our communities. We should leave restaurants with empty pockets and healthy appreciation of the people who struggle to make a living in the service industry."

If you find yourself not wanting to leave a tip, think about your decision. Your server might be a young minister trying to earn enough money to take care of his newborn son. I do not mean to harp on this point, but leaving no tip is unacceptable. As Christians, followers of Christ, we should be the most generous people on earth. We should give freely, as Christ gives to us.

At some point, the father made the connection between my sermon and his treatment of me the previous evening. At the end of my sermon, he gathered his family and crept out the back door. He did not return or apologize, probably because my message that day was "unacceptable".

DON'T EVEN THINK ABOUT IT

Speaking of acceptable, a sweet couple came to the restaurant one night to celebrate reaching twenty-five years of marriage. It was a pleasure to serve them. Upon their arrival, I greeted them with glasses of champagne. The chef sent a few special appetizers to the table. After clearing their dinner plates, I had the pastry chef create a special dessert to celebrate the couple. From my perspective, the service, meal and atmosphere were first-rate. The couple had a wonderful evening. I was certain they would leave a fat tip.

Instead of leaving real money, however, they left a copy of the New Testament with a fake one-hundred-dollar bill inside. Written on the fake Ben Franklin was a message glorifying eternal salvation through Jesus Christ. I was furious with Eric Evangelical for leaving the precious gift of eternal salvation. He didn't know I was also an ordained minister hustling for tips, and he was apparently unaware that I need tips—actual money —to provide for my family. I applauded Mr. Evangelical for boldly sharing his Christian faith, but someone needed to tell him it's imperative to crack out a cash tip to accompany such blatant Christian propaganda. Some other information that might behoove him is that in America, servers and bartenders receive the majority of their income through gratuity. Restaurants cannot force customers to leave a tip, but tipping is a well-established custom.

Casting professional etiquette aside, I hustled to the lobby to ask him if there had been an issue with my service. A professional server at a five-star restaurant should never confront a customer about the appropriateness of their tip, but despite my distasteful behavior, I was hoping my brother in Christ had just made a simple mistake.

"Excuse me, sir, I appreciate the pamphlet you left at the table, but I noticed you did not leave a tip. Was there something wrong with my service?"

Mr. Evangelical was somewhat perplexed by the question. Gathering his words, he said, "There is no greater tip than salvation through Jesus Christ."

Buttons were pushed. I struggled to hold it together. "Sir, a better tip would have been real money, because I am certain the twenty times I rededicated my life to Christ in high school is still acceptable to our Lord and Savior. As a matter of fact, I've been so captivated by the teachings of Jesus, I became an ordained minister. I work at the restaurant part-time because my sweet little church doesn't have the resources to afford a full-time associate minister. I depend on the generosity of customers like yourself to support my family."

At this awkward moment, I was not expecting Mr. Evangelical to reach into his pocket to offer a cash tip, but it would have been a pleasant surprise. He remained stoic to a hard-working minister's plea and powered on by offering this nugget of joy —"What a blessing to share the saving power of Jesus Christ with your coworkers who are facing the wages of sin. I know you will find a wayward soul who needs to encounter the power of the Risen Christ. I believe the Lord will continue to bless your ministry."

Listen carefully—do not be this type of Christian. As Americans, we are blessed with the freedom to share our faith. When you share your Christian faith with people in the service industry, please bless these hard workers with money. Leave as many Bibles as you like. Tell the world about the amazing church you attend. But do not use evangelism as an excuse not to bless someone financially.

As the modern church moves towards a post-Christian culture, it's essential to write Jesus's name upon our hearts. "By this everyone will know that you are my disciples, if you love one another (John 13:35)." A faithful Christian must be known for compassion, not a misperception of conservative politics. A generous tip is one of the best ways to love people in the service industry. No one wants to be considered stingy.

A few extra dollars can be the difference between a good tip and a great tip. Last time our family dined at the Waffle House, our entire bill was twenty dollars. I've been to numerous bars and restaurants in Los Angeles where a single cocktail costs twenty dollars. At the Waffle House, we left the waitress a twenty-dollar tip. At first, she thought our family made a mistake and tried to return the money. There was no mistake, we just wanted this woman to feel loved.

YOU POURED TOO MUCH

I am a firm believer that every able-bodied American should be required to work at least one year in the service industry. It is said that we learn everything about life in kindergarten. However, restaurants teach employees how to practice patience, respect and gratitude for other people. Service to others is another important lesson many are missing these days. Waiting on customers for one year can teach a person everything there is to know about respecting other people.

At the bar one night, a female customer began to frantically wave her arms. Hustling over to assist her, I asked with a smile, "Is everything alright?"

"No, everything is not alright!" she seethed. "You filled my glass with too much wine." She offered this frivolous complaint with a sour expression.

Taking the high road, I replied, "I am really sorry. It was the end of the bottle, and I poured a little heavy instead of throwing away the bottle."

Normally, this would have been the end of the discussion. Case closed. Move on to the next mystery. This woman, however, was not someone to be trifled with.

"Young man, you have poured too much wine. Within the next twenty minutes, I will drink too much wine and become drunk. This unacceptable behavior will be your fault. For the past ten years, I have restricted myself to one glass of wine per night. As we can both see, this is more than one simple glass of wine."

A little confused, I resorted to simple logic. "You don't have to drink the entire glass."

Not caring for my response, she continued her rather absurd

complaint. "Well, that would be wasteful. If you would have poured the proper amount of wine the first time, we would not be having this discussion."

As a result, I offered two simple solutions—I could pour some of the wine down the drain or drink some of it for her. This attempt at humor didn't change her expression in the slightest. Eventually, we gave her glass of wine to another patron, one who thoroughly enjoyed the generous overpour. I then poured a fresh glass of wine with the proper amount of alcohol for her desired level of consumption.

Life lessons like this serve as a reminder that some people spend their lives searching for reasons to complain. A world focused on discontent dismisses Jesus's desire to establish the kingdom of heaven.

PREACHER MAN

Last summer, I encountered an unexpected and prolonged spiritual attack. The evening began in an ordinary way. The restaurant opened and people began to fill seats at the bar. I walked to the end of the bar and asked a young woman if she would like to order a drink. After chewing the fat for a few minutes, one of the servers said, "Hey, Preacher Man! I need a lemon drop martini." After making the martini, I returned to take the young woman's order, but there was one major problem—she was loaded for bear. She was outraged that an upscale restaurant would hire a minister to serve cocktails. Spewing bitterness, she said, "I bet you think I'm going straight to hell because I'm an atheist. Maybe if I stay at the bar long enough, I will be washed by the blood of Christ."

The night I got chewed out for not eating a marijuana-laced gummy at a friend's wedding came to mind. Here we go again. Her words were designed to elicit a negative response. We stared at one another for a few moments until she finally broke the silence. "Some people are so stupid to believe in Jesus."

Nothing constructive would be gained by engaging this young woman in a theological conversation. Other ministers might disagree with my approach, but this customer was carrying deep spiritual wounds; wounds too deep to address at the local bar. She was not seeking the comfort of Bible verses or the assurance of salvation through Jesus Christ. This woman had been spiritually wounded by the Christian faith. Behind the mask of sarcasm, her soul was longing for God's immense love, grace and compassion.

Borrowing from a vast inventory of bartender and pastoral wisdom, I said, "Thank you for inviting me into this difficult conversation. I hope you find the answers you're seeking."

To my surprise, these benign words were like spilling gasoline onto a smoldering fire. In the middle of helping another customer, the disenchanted young lady launched a vicious verbal sparring match. I meant it sincerely, but she had apparently interpreted it as condescending sarcasm.

It was clear this customer was angry and looking for a target on whom to unload her spiritual wrath. She needed an outlet to express her frustration with the Christian faith. Upon returning to her end of the bar, she began yelling to anyone willing to listen.

"Hey, everyone! The bartending preacher thinks we're all going to burn in hell. Go ahead and order another drink, unless you think he is serving you the blood of Christ."

Thankfully, a regular at the bar became my protector.

"Andy has been nothing but respectful. I can't listen to you attack him any longer. He's not trying to provoke a fight. Now I'm upset because you're ruining my dinner."

At this point, the woman slapped a twenty on the bar and called out, "I hope everyone is happy with this hypocrite behind the bar."

Wait a second—our manager hired a hypocrite? Why am I always the last to know?

STOP CALLING ME A TENT BUILDER

Readers of the Bible first encounter the Apostle Paul in the book of Acts, which details the spread of Christianity at the conclusion of Jesus's ministry. Paul never met Jesus in person, instead proclaiming a Divine encounter on the road to Damascus. After witnessing an image of the risen Christ, Paul devoted his life to preaching the love, grace and mercy of Jesus Christ. But there's a catch—in the early part of Paul's ministry, he supported himself as a tentmaker. Instead of navigating a delicate balance between bartender and minister, the Apostle Paul was busy helping his friends get packed for a weekend camping trip.

Seeking to make a biblical connection, church members have referred to my work at the restaurant as tent-building. Yes, this is an elegant method for making sense of my two professions. However, Paul was not saving money for his kid's college fund, nor was he planning a Hawaiian vacation to celebrate his tenth anniversary with his wife. As a matter of fact, Paul pursued the gift of celibacy; a gift I have never sought. Additionally, it is a gift that costs much less than bicycles, video games, and dollhouses.

I am not saying Paul didn't need the money, but I don't think he was hustling for tips. Life was not easy for the apostle; numerous times he was beaten, ridiculed, and put in jail for professing faith in the Risen Christ. But when he hit the mean streets of Tarsus, he was blessed with the opportunity to serve as his own boss. He set his own hours and prices and wielded the power to refuse service to anyone. It's entirely plausible that our bold Christian forefather told rude customers to hit the

road. There is something beautiful about financial inde-
pendence.

If you ask my children what I do for a living, they will tell you I
am a bartender. They know I work for a church, but they believe I
mix cocktails to support our family. To make matters worse, our
daughter believes I go church just to ask people for money.
Through her eyes, I roll through the aisles pleading for money
until some poor sap throws out a twenty-dollar bill to make the
embarrassing episode disappear. It's interesting that a ten-year-old
has made a powerful connection between the church and money.

I am not even sure where she developed this idea. Yes, the
church does have to discuss finances and raise a budget. But as
the associate minister, I've never been tasked with asking
church members for money. However, I upset a few church
curmudgeons when I sold an ugly Christmas sweater for five-
hundred dollars at the Christmas Eve service. Even on this
night, the proceeds did not find their way into the church
offering plate. The ugly sweater money was donated to a local
non-profit which serves at-risk youth.

STICK TO THE SCRIPT

As we navigate life together, it is important to stick to the script.
No one really cares that I worked as a busboy for close to three
years before I was allowed to pour mixed drinks. Going rogue
might seem brave, but it can generate a host of unforeseen
issues. A few years back, I went off-script on a cross-country
flight. The script read, "I work in a restaurant in Colorado." If I
would have said that, it would have been the end of the discussion, and we would have then been free to pull out books and
ignore each other for the duration of the flight. On this particular flight, however, to make things more interesting, I claimed
to be a certified public accountant. Bold-faced lies are never the

path to freedom, especially when you get busted. My accounting career took a nosedive on take-off.

Much to my chagrin, this passenger was the world's most enthusiastic accountant. Enthusiastic number-lovers are thought to be mythical creatures, like unicorns, but I found one. This passionate man worshipped numbers as a Chief Financial Officer for an international Christian non-profit. I was cornered. Trapped.

There were three natural solutions at this point—continue the lie, tell the truth, or fake motion sickness. The little angel on my shoulder said it was too late to fake motion sickness, so I looked the eager beaver accountant in the eyes and said, "Wait. What? I'm not an accountant. Why did I even say that?"

The ship was sinking quickly. Returning to the script provided the best opportunity to save face. I apologized for the confusion, then offered a half-truth.

"I hustle for tips at a high-end steak house."

Thankfully, my brand-new CPA friend did not want to talk about cash tips or the price of steak.

FAITHFUL

For those who are unaware, quitting a lucrative restaurant job is akin to breaking a bad habit. You say to yourself, "I'll just work one more shift and then I'll be done for good." Or maybe you try to sneak a shift or two when the wife and kids are on vacation. You begin to tell yourself lies, "One extra shift never hurt anyone." Next thing you know, you're sixty years old sneaking shifts at the local Applebee's because you think no one is watching. Yet, church members, God and the IRS are always watching.

In 2015, I gathered the courage to quit the restaurant. I puffed up my chest, entered the general manager's office and provided a solid two-weeks' notice. The job had been a blessing to my family. It provided enough money to cover the bills and take the kids on fun trips. Despite the benefits and camaraderie, though, it was time to pursue full-time ministry. Full of confidence and vigor, I launched into my speech. "Thank you for all of the love and support, but it's time to move on. Y'all have been so good to my family and ministry. Dodi and I would not have survived our first year in Colorado without the restaurant. After weeks of soul-searching, it has become apparent that I will not be able to move into full-time ministry until I kick my part-time restaurant habit." Satisfied with my impassioned speech, I turned on my heels and walked out the front door.

It's been six years since I submitted my two weeks' notice, and I'm still sticking it to the man by clocking two to three nights a week at the restaurant. The answer is simple, I stay because the job offers the money and flexibility to support our family. Through the birth of children, the loss of income, and a dozen other vicissitudes, the restaurant remains steadfast.

BEING BROKE IS NOT A BLESSING

In April of 2012, exactly a month before our son was born, our sweet little church began to experience financial difficulties. In layman's terms, the church was broke and could no longer afford my part-time salary. This is not the joyous news I wanted to share with my pregnant wife and two-year-old daughter. A pregnant woman does not need additional stress. Looking back, the difficult situation felt like a swift donkey kick to the face.

Our leadership team planned to restore my salary as soon as the church was financially able. In the interim, I needed to find an alternate method to earn a paycheck. Putting a positive spin on a negative situation, the church bookkeeper said, "Andy, this is an exciting time of growth. As a result, the church is facing some financial challenges and opportunities. God is testing us, and we must respond with great faith."

I understand faith, but last time I checked, American Express needs cold, hard cash to cover the bill, not faith in Jesus Christ.

Because anxiety and stress are the two most common emotions when people can't pay their bills, I've never viewed financial challenges and opportunities as "exciting." When I was a kid, people who couldn't afford groceries, rent or gas money were considered broke. It meant there was no money in the piggy bank to pay for that Snickers bar. That situation is frightening, not exciting.

PRAYER CHANGES US

With a great sense of desperation, Dodi and I got down on our knees and cried out in prayer. We pondered moving back to Georgia or North Carolina to live with our parents. I considered leaving the ministry to pursue a job at a local ski shop. Friends in California offered us a free place to live. Though friends and family surrounded us with love and support, the situation felt desperate. We had no idea what to do.

After many long discussions and restless nights, we decided to stay in Colorado. To make finances work, I begged the restaurant for full-time hours. Without hesitation, our general manager created extra shifts in the work schedule. Within a few days, two nights a week became five nights a week. To fill the extra hours, I picked up shifts as a busboy, bar-back and food runner. To support our young family, I was willing to work any position offered.

It was a stressful season filled with numerous challenges and opportunities, but our family was blessed through God's provision. The restaurant surrounded our family with love and support. The church kept a roof over our heads. And God's people shared extra food, clothes, and finances. Approximately a year later, I returned to the church on a part-time basis and scaled back to a few shifts a week at the restaurant.

Life in Colorado has been completely different than we ever imagined. It has been filled with lots of vegans, puffy coats, and personal struggles. Yet, my coworkers at the restaurant have become a second family. As extended family, we've mourned the loss of parents, battled unbearable addictions, and celebrated the birth of children. In the winter, we have spent countless mornings skiing at the resort together. At work a few hours later, we set aside moments to recall the best parts of the day. We remember the amazing tree skiing off the top of chair nine. We talk about the terrible conditions in Revelation Bowl. Most important, we swear to never grow up and get real jobs.

On beautiful summer nights, before everyone gets too rowdy, we make plans to mountain bike, paddle board, hike 14,000-foot peaks, and explore the National Forest. On days off, we attend festivals, play softball, and cheer for the Denver Broncos. Most important, we laugh until our stomachs hurt.

When the demons of drugs and alcohol start to wreck our lives, we step in to offer support. We circle the wagons when people experience heart break. When a housing crisis occurs, a co-worker is quick to offer a couch or laundry room to share. If you want to know why I stay, it's because these people are written in my heart.

At forty-two years of age, it's hard to believe I hustle two part-time jobs. In my deluded mind, I could end the part-time hustle with a full-time job at a Texas mega-church. I am not sure if this is true, but it's the story I like to tell. With the added income and job security, we could buy a nice house with a two-car garage in the suburbs. Our kids could attend prestigious private schools. On Christmas morning, our house would be filled with more presents than we'd have time to open.

But would our family be happy? Would I be happy? These are the big questions. More money is not going to make me a better husband or father. One stable job is not going to improve my family's quality of life. For the past ten years, adventure and quality time with family has served as life's barometer. At this stage of life, the water glass continues to remain half-full. When it becomes half-empty, my family will consider making a change. Until we reach that point, though, I'll remain content snowboarding on Monday, pouring drinks on Saturday, and preaching on Sunday.

CHAPTER 17

EXPERIENCE CHANGES EVERYTHING

"Before you judge a man, walk a mile in his shoes. After that who cares? ...He's a mile away and you've got his shoes!"— Billy Connolly

AT LEAST BRUSH YOUR TEETH

If we remain open to the experience, our lives will be transformed. Sometimes all it takes is a simple invitation for the transformation to begin. It was early on Sunday morning when one of line cooks stumbled into the sanctuary. Twenty minutes after the service began, he staggered through the aisles reeking of alcohol and cigarettes. He spotted our family and dropped into the pew next to our son. For years, this young man had struggled with drugs and alcohol. His painful addictions pushed him to the margins of society. From Jesus's perspective, this young man is a beloved child of God.

Life is not about getting everything right but, rather, a willingness to embrace the invitation. Esteemed theologian Stanley Hauerwas wrote, "The difference between followers of Jesus and those who do not know Jesus is that those who have seen Jesus no longer have any excuse to avoid 'the least of these.'"[1]

Many people floating on the periphery of life qualify as *the least of these.*

In this earthly realm, the righteous are those who take care of God's children without expecting anything in return. Jesus teaches a simple way to care for the world when he proclaims, "I was hungry, and you gave Me *something* to eat; I was thirsty, and you gave Me *something* to drink; I was a stranger, and you invited Me in; naked, and you clothed Me; I was sick, and you visited Me; I was in prison, and you came to Me." (Matthew 25: 35-36). If someone truly loves and honors Jesus, their actions will display this love.

REAL ALIENS LIVE IN OUTER SPACE

It's easy to voice negative opinions about illegal immigrants. That is, until one or more becomes your friend. During the years working in the restaurant industry, I have encountered numerous young men and women who entered the United States illegally. Most of these document-ally challenged coworkers were brought to this country as young children by their parents.

One coworker recalled a particularly harrowing experience as a five-year-old boy living in Mexico. In the middle of the night, his mother crept into his bedroom to begin their escape from an abusive father. She put her hand over his mouth and guided him out the rear window into the alley behind their house. Without an overnight bag and his beloved stuffed animal, he was told to run without looking back. Filled with fear and out of breath, they jumped into their uncle's waiting car. They drove three hours to the US-Mexico border. Without notice, the uncle pulled over, and mother and son were forced out of the car and onto the side of the road.

Shortly before daybreak, they jumped into the Rio Grande in search of a new life. The strong current pulled them downstream, but they were determined to reach the safety of the American border. Struggling through the surging water, the terrified mother and child finally pulled themselves onto the safety of the Texas riverbank. Soaking wet, the brave mother wrapped her loving arms around her youngest child as they waited. They did not know what to expect, but men had been paid to deliver the family to safety.

After a long moment of silence, strangers exited the shadows and descended upon the young family. Mother and son were able to cross the dangerous river, but their journey was just beginning. Two strange men began shouting and then hurried to collect the family. Without a proper introduction, they were shuttled into the back of an old delivery van. Inside, they joined twenty more men, women and children searching for a new American beginning.

For the next twenty-four hours, everyone rode in dark silence until they arrived in Colorado. Without notice, the van came to a screeching halt. The rear door rolled open and everyone was pulled out. Standing in a deserted parking lot, another round of bargaining began to take place. My friend still didn't know what was happening, then he and a few other children were put into the back of an old pickup truck. Within a few hours, his harrowing journey would be complete.

Yes, this young man was brought to this country illegally, but he has lived as an American for over twenty years. Some people believe he should be deported to Mexico, a country where his abusive biological father still lives. He was brought to the United States before starting kindergarten, yet many people believe this grown man should be returned to a country where he has no friends or memories.

Before he reached an age of accountability, his mother brought him to the United States. He was raised in an English-speaking community and graduated high school with honors. He works hard and pays taxes. Not once has he been involved in any illegal activities. He is married to an illegal immigrant. Together, the couple is raising their American-born son. Based on current laws, my friend and his wife could be deported, but his son would be allowed to stay in the United States.

Again, it is easy to voice strong opinions against illegal immigrants until one of them becomes your friend. As an American citizen, I don't know how to respond to the millions of immigrants who want to cross our border. But as a Christian, I know we must embrace and love our neighbors who live outside our country. Jesus clearly tells his followers to love our neighbors as we love ourselves. I do not know how to solve this challenge. However, I do know we are called to love these people.

Over the years, I've never heard a minister call Jesus or his family illegal immigrants. Mary, Joseph, and everyone in their Egyptian caravan were undocumented workers. They did not ask Pharaoh for asylum. Instead, they packed their belongings and crossed the Egyptian border to escape persecution. Egypt was a part of the Roman Empire, but the caravan did not seek permission from their local government to relocate.

Before fleeing Judea, Jesus's family did not apply for work visas, social security numbers, or passports. Despite this interesting narrative in the life of Christ, no one calls Joseph an undocumented worker. Would anyone in our churches dare call Jesus or his family illegal residents? Just like many illegal immigrants living in the United States today, Jesus's family depended on the safety of a foreign country to protect them from violence.

I am not trying to solve legal and illegal immigration. I am calling on our nation to embrace the plight of the outcast, the foreigner, and the immigrant. As Christians, we must discern ways to extend grace and compassion to modern immigrants. We must address the deeper question, "Why are people fleeing their home countries for the safety of the United States?"

Instead of building a wall, the American government should explore avenues to create safer environments within the home countries of our nation's illegal immigrants so that fewer will want or need to flee in the night, swim across frigid rivers with their children, risk abuse at the hands of coyotes (transporters), and leave everything and everyone they've ever known behind to have a small piece of what most of us take for granted.

CHAPTER 18

POST-GLADIATOR FAME

"This is television, that's all it is. It has nothing to do with people, it's to do with ratings! For fifty years, we've told them what to eat, what to drink, what to wear...for Christ's sake, Ben, don't you understand? Americans love television. They wean their kids on it. Listen. They love game shows, they love wrestling, they love sports and violence. So what do we do? We give 'em what they want! We're number one, Ben! That's all that counts, believe me. I've been in the business for thirty years." —Richard Dawson as Damon Killian in The Running Man (1987)

LIFE AFTERWARDS

Years after my appearance on *American Gladiator*, coworkers at the restaurant still called me Gladiator. It was an amazing experience, but it is not the moment I wanted to define my life. Thankfully, I have been able to parlay *American Gladiator* fame into other opportunities, including an invitation in 2014 to compete on *American Ninja Warrior*.

Before competing, I could not comprehend the evolving *Ninja Warrior* subculture. Men and women across the country build obstacles and train together. They live, eat and breathe competing on *Ninja Warrior*. Standing backstage, I discovered my lack of preparation for the event. Competitors knew the specific names and dimensions of obstacles. They shared tips and techniques for completing the difficult course.

To be the best, you must specifically train to be the best. For example, to become a better tennis player, you must practice all aspects of the game—your forehand, backhand, and serve. When you're not on the court, you're in the weight room improving your strength and flexibility. At home, you focus on nutrition, rest and mental preparedness. A professional tennis player can complete on *Ninja Warrior,* but they will never rise to the top if they are not completely dedicated to becoming a Ninja.

WHAT HAPPENED NEXT?

Ninja Warrior is filmed in the middle of the night because darkness creates better lighting for the cameras. I was not scheduled to run the course until three a.m. Despite the late start time, Ninjas are required to be on set at sundown and remain on set until sunrise. Hours after arriving to compete, I ascended the platform, ready to challenge the course. Sitting in the audience less than fifty feet away was my sweet young family. At the time, my little girl, Emmi Claire, was four, and our little boy, Crew, was two. As one might expect, the obstacles looked easier when I was sitting at home.

With false confidence, I breezed through the first four obstacles. Full of assurance, vigor and adrenaline, I reached the fifth obstacle, the Devil's Steps, an upside-down staircase suspended twenty feet over a shallow pool of water. It's designed so that competitors must use only their hands to climb the undercarriage of the stairs. After climbing up, competitors must traverse a six-foot gap using only their arms and grip strength. After crossing the gap, aspiring ninjas descend the steps and head toward the next obstacle standing in their way.

With great trepidation, I scaled the first seven steps and reached the top. Upon reaching the gap, the distance between steps looked impossible to cross. Holding on with my right hand, I swung my left arm across the gap. My fingers brushed the opposite side, at which point I lost balance and tumbled into the water below.

Climbing out of the pool soaking wet, a commentator pulled me aside and asked, "Andy, what happened?"

There wasn't much to say. I didn't make it. I fell into the water. As we were returning to our hotel, Emmi Claire said, "It's okay, Dad. I'm still proud of you."

Despite the failure, being a hero to my family was well worth the effort. There is nothing wrong with failure, but to move forward in life, we cannot allow ourselves to be afraid of it. How we embrace failure as we navigate life is under our control. We can see failure as the end of the world, or we can see it as an invaluable learning experience.

The esteemed American inventor Thomas Edison once said regarding the invention of the lightbulb, "I have not failed. I've just found ten thousand ways that won't work." Every failure is an opportunity for growth. As we embrace failure, we create a system for avoiding the same mistakes. Remember, failure will only stop us if we let it.

Despite encountering failures on *American Gladiators* and *Ninja Warrior*, I continue to challenge myself as an athlete, father and minister. I continue to train, preparing myself mentally and physically for the next adventure. I would rather fail than miss an amazing opportunity because I was unprepared.

RULES CHANGE

When you decide to play a game—any game—remember that the decision-makers have the power to change the rules. After a game is invented, it often evolves and transforms. In 1906, American football legalized the forward pass. Later, in 1933, a passer could throw the ball from anywhere behind the line of scrimmage. This particular rule change made quarterback the most important position on the field. In 1954, the National Basketball Association introduced the shot clock. Scoring increased by more than ten points per game during the inaugural season. On January 11, 1973, Major League baseball team owners granted American League teams the right to use a designated hitter to bat for the pitcher. Owners, managers, and players believed the designated hitter would generate more run-scoring opportunities. With the change, American League pitchers would no longer be required to dig in at home plate. This new rule adoption made a clear distinction between the American and National leagues.

I am not a professional athlete, but the rules changed after flying to Los Angeles in November of 2018, to compete on a new CBS show called *Million Dollar Mile*. For the purpose of the show, everyday athletes were invited to compete for a chance to win a million dollars. Standing in the athletes' way was a challenging obstacle course filled with a group of elite racers conspiring to stop competitors from winning money at all costs.

On the night I was invited to run the course, competitors were given a two-minute head start to complete as many obstacles as possible, but they had to escape the game without being caught by a defender. As originally structured, each completed obstacle had an assigned monetary value. The first obstacle was worth $10,000, the second $25,000, the third $50,000, the fourth $100,000, and the fifth $250,000. To keep their money, contestants had to leave the game by completing the exit obstacle without being caught. If captured by a defender, contestants would earn nothing, no matter how many obstacles they completed beforehand. Competitors who were able to complete all five obstacles without being caught were given the opportunity to keep $250,000, or risk everything for a chance at a million dollars.

Upon hearing these rules, I told the producers no one would risk everything to go for the million-dollar prize. One of the producers glared at me and said, "You're out of your mind. Of course, somebody will go for a million dollars."

Without overthinking my response, I said, "You're out of *your* mind. There is no way I'm going for a million if I've already pocketed $250,000. I can't go for a million, knowing I'll go home with nothing if I fail. I can't imagine someone taking that kind of risk. If I told my wife I lost $250,000 trying to win a million, I better *not* come home."

It's easy to say $250,000 is not life-changing money, but paying off the mortgage and sending Bubba and Betsy Mae to college sure is. Conversely, coming home with nothing would be life-changing as well, and not in a good way. I can't begin to fathom the regret of leaving that kind of money on the table.

During the second night of filming, sixteen runners were anxiously waiting backstage for the opportunity to compete. Before anyone was allowed to run, the producers came backstage to restate the rules. On the night I was scheduled to run, runners would be granted a two-minute head start. However, the head start time could be changed based upon the producer's discretion. Second, to receive money, runners had to leave the game without being caught.

Before leaving the room, a member of the production team said, "Runners, if you choose to run tonight, these are the rules. Remember, these are the rules *right now*. These rules could change tomorrow or even later tonight based upon results.

Based upon the current rules given, you have the right to decline your invitation to take the course. Just remember, if you decline the chance to compete tonight, there is no guarantee you will be given a second chance to run the course. We want everybody to run, but you might not get a chance."

After the speech about rules, a producer said, "If anyone is willing to attempt our featured obstacle tonight—Deep Water Solo—we guarantee you will run tonight. But you must begin with the featured obstacle."

Based upon the layout of the course, runners were able to select the order of their obstacles. Initially, Deep Water Solo was penciled in as my second obstacle. Not wanting to miss the opportunity to compete, I decided to rearrange my original plan and challenge the defender and on the featured obstacle.

Several hours later, I was brought on stage to meet the host of the show, Tim Tebow. Upon meeting, I was asked "Andy, what's your goal?"

"My goal is to win enough money to take my wife on an amazing tenth anniversary trip, and to support two of our favorite organizations, Habitat for Humanity and World Vision."

After answering all of Tebow's questions, it was time to meet my defender, Veejay Jones. Nicknamed The Prodigy, Jones is the youngest Spartan Race winner in history. This young man was hoping to crush a poor minister's dreams of winning money.

Armed with a two-minute head start, Tebow yelled, "Go!"

Let's be honest about what happened. I was a little jacked-up and came out of the gates too hot. The distance between obstacles was roughly a quarter mile, which means runners must preserve their energy by running long distance speed, not sprint speed. By the time I reached Deep Water Solo, which was less than a mile away, I was already breathing heavy. That was no time to hesitate. I had to dive into the pool and charge ahead to the overhanging and gigantic climbing holds. Cold and soaked with water, I scrambled over them and exited the obstacle.

At this point, runners would return to the center of the game called The Hub, where runners had to decide if they wanted to face another pre-selected obstacle or leave the game. According to the rules in place when I ran the course, players had to exit the game without being caught to win money. If you were caught on the course, you would not win any money, no matter how many obstacles you completed.

These were the rules, and they clearly stated if you get caught by the defender, you win nothing. It doesn't matter how many obstacles you completed; you must return unscathed to Tim Tebow. Armed with the game rules and a general understanding of the obstacles, I formed a plan. Complete two obstacles, win $25,000 and exit the game.

It is essential to understand that the Defenders had been practicing the obstacles and running the course for several weeks before the Runners arrived in California. This must be repeated, Runners weren't allowed to test any of the obstacles before running the course. We were only allowed to view a demonstration of the obstacle. The producers would not even allow the Runners to touch the obstacles.

STICK TO THE PLAN

Before walking onstage to meet Tim Tebow, I repeated my mantra, "Stick to the plan, two obstacles and out. Two obstacles and out. Do not deviate from the plan." To ensure a victory, it was essential to stick to the plan. If I deviated from the original plan by chasing after bigger prize money, there was a strong chance I would come home empty-handed.

Deep Water Solo was much harder than I expected. The Defender was closing the gap. I could press my luck and head to my second obstacle called Spiraling Up, or I could head for the exit obstacle with hopes of bringing home $10,000. At the Hub, I made the decision to exit the game.

Exiting the game after completing Deep Water Solo was not the best experience for television viewers, but $10,000 is a lot of money for a minister. Before collecting any money, I still had to complete a fifteen-story rope climb up the side of a slick, cement office building. I hustled over to the safety harness and feverishly scrambled up the side of the office building. Looking over my shoulder, I could see the Defender known as The Prodigy vigorously climbing the rope. Less than ten feet from the top of the rope climb, my triceps and biceps were screaming with fatigue. Upon surveying the short distance, I willed my arms to pull my heavy body to victory. The last few inches were agonizing as I pawed at the rope to finish. The last few seconds were agonizing, but a few moments later, I swung my legs over the top of the fifteen-story building.

The chase for the money was over. It was time to descend the 300-foot zipline back to center stage. Upon arriving, Tim Tebow said, "Andy, you still had a minute-twenty lead on your defender. Why didn't you keep going?"

Somewhat shocked, I replied "He shaved off forty seconds in the first obstacle."

If I'm doing my math right, that means I would've completed the second obstacle—Spiraling Up—with maybe thirty-second lead before heading over to the exit obstacle. I refused to leave money on the table, I could not bear the thought of coming home empty-handed.

The night before running the course, I told my wife, "I am coming home with money; it's just a matter of how much." In the past ten years, I have received goose eggs on two Nationally syndicated televisions shows, *American Gladiators* and *Ninja Warrior*. In my third and possibly final game show appearance, I was bound and determined to come home with cold, hard cash.

Full of confidence, I looked Tebow in the eyes, "He would've caught me. My mama knew he was going to catch me. (Pointing to the Defender.) He knew he was going to catch me. You knew he was going to catch me. Everyone knew."

I looked over at my twenty-year-old Defender, and he agreed, "I would've caught you."

Maybe I would have made it through the two obstacles without being caught, but that was just a maybe. After the show aired, I asked my best friend from childhood, "Do you think I would have made it through two obstacles without being caught?"

"Not a chance," he replied. "I told my coworkers you were too smart to come home without any money. Watching that defender, I knew you would have been caught on the second obstacle."

Answers like this remind everyone why we have best friends; they keep us humble.

THE PLOT THICKENS

For an interesting plot twist, which I discovered post-production: The rules of the game changed after I ran the course; something the producers of the show were very clear could take place. The next evening, runners were allowed to keep half of their winnings if they were caught trying to complete their next obstacle. For example, if a runner completed the $25,000 obstacle and were caught by the defender on the $50,000 obstacle, runners would still win half the money from the highest obstacle completed. This rule change encouraged runners to attempt more obstacles because they were assured to win money even if they were caught by their Defender. It was a savvy move by the production team, but different rules from those under which I competed.

If I would have been offered this new set of rules, I would have played the game until I was caught by my Defender. There would have been zero hesitation about continuing the game after completing the first obstacle. Yes, a large part of my decision to leave the game after completing just one obstacle was the fear of failure, and for the past ten years, friends and strangers have found a need to remind the world about my loss on *American Gladiators*. Nothing in life's little handbook can prepare an individual for losing money in front of millions of people. As a result, I refused to face criticism for another ten years if I did not come home with money from the *Million Dollar Mile*.

FEAR NOT

Despite Jesus's pleas for his followers to abandon fear, I was letting an irrational fear of failure guide my decisions. In Luke 12:22-24, Jesus gathers his beloved companions and says, "Do not worry about your life, as to what you will eat; nor for your body, as to what you will put on.[23] For life is more than food, and the body more than clothing. [24] Consider the ravens, for they neither sow nor reap; they have no storeroom nor barn, and yet God feeds them; how much more valuable you are than the birds!"

Jesus's earliest followers were living under the oppression of the Roman Empire, a ruling class willing to destroy anyone or anything standing in their way. I, on the other hand, was afraid of losing a game.

We cannot live our lives in fear of failure. Therefore, it is imperative to have a plan. Maybe you will not be invited to compete on a television show, but you will face major events in life. When these events arise, it is imperative to be ready with a plan. Yes, I deviated from my original plan, but I achieved my goal of returning to Colorado with money for my family. In life, we must have a plan in place before we encounter big moments.

Just remember the old saying—if you're failing to plan, you're planning to fail.

I'VE BEEN HERE BEFORE

As the runners were sitting backstage mentally preparing to run the course, another competitor was talking a big game about taking home the million-dollar prize. His plan: finish all the obstacles, beat the Defender, and walk home with a fat paycheck. *Great if that's your plan,* I thought, *but that's not my plan.*

He had a plan, but it was a plan built on hype. He was all jacked-up, making his fellow runners anxious with toxic energy. For several hours, he was barking backstage, "I don't care what happens. I came here for the money, and I plan to take it all."

Just remember, if you're about to get into a fight and the other person seems way too calm, you better walk away or form a new plan. Why? Because this calm individual has a reason to be calm. My reason, I have been in the spotlight before. I have suffered a major loss. I have battled numerous injuries. But most important, I know what it takes to win money on national television. I had a plan, and by gosh, I was going to execute the plan.

As for the guy talking the big game about winning a million dollars, he changed his plan. After confidently strutting onto stage, he followed my advice by finishing one obstacle and heading for the exit. No, he did not come close to winning a million dollars, but he did take $10,000 home to his family.

As a matter of fact, not a single runner even attempted the million-dollar obstacle. The game was too hard, and the Defenders were too strong. Nobody won the million-dollar prize. One runner, a professional paddle boarder, walked home with a quarter of a million dollars.

CHAPTER 19

DR. PEPPER

"Wouldn't it have been weird to go to high school with the Pope? You know, somebody did, someone's sitting at home, watching TV in Poland, they see the Pope, they think, "That guy was a jerk! He was so mean to me and now he's Pope? I got a swirly from the Pope!"—Jim Gaffigan

SISYPHUS

As a student, I've always felt like Sisyphus, a heartless king found in Greek Mythology. Zeus condemned Sisyphus to eternal punishment as a result of the king's insidious behavior. To repay his grievous actions, the evil king was forced to push a giant boulder up a steep mountain until the end of time. At the very top of the mountain, the boulder would tumble back to the bottom. At this point, Sisyphus would trudge back down the mountain to push the boulder back uphill again.

Throughout my scholastic career, academic achievements and milestones have stood as massive boulders I've been forced to push uphill for eternity. At every step, daunting mountain-tops loomed on the horizon. In elementary school, reading one page from Dr. Seuss's *Green Eggs and Ham* was a monumental task. In middle school, understanding the simple concepts of pre-algebra became kryptonite. As a high school student, my writing problems became exponentially problematic when I was required to take a foreign language. In college, more than one professor was appalled with my improper use of grammar and punctuation. In seminary, a biblical Greek professor was shocked to hear that I had never learned to diagram a sentence. Despite all of these challenges, I was able to graduate college and earn a Master of Divinity.

The vast majority of my academic achievements would not have been possible without The Individuals with Disabilities Education Act (IDEA). This act was first established in 1975 and was called the Education of Handicapped Children Act. These laws provide schools, colleges, and universities with academic guidelines to address the unique needs of students with disabilities.

As a result of the Disability Act, I was assigned notetakers during college and seminary. Free tutors were available to help with studies. Extended time on exams and written assignments was offered for every class except for art and drama. Seminary professors were made aware of my special needs and offered one-on-one instruction after class. Thank God for all of this special help. Without the support of family and schools, I would not have graduated high school, college, or seminary.

In 2008, I graduated Fuller Seminary with a Master in Divinity, a goal the majority of my high school teachers would have been astonished to learn. Not only did I earn a master's degree, but this problematic hyperactive teenager had studied to become a minister. This academic journey was not the one anyone could have predicted.

After Seminary graduation, I was convinced my academic journey was over. I had completed more as a student than I ever thought possible. A large portion of college and seminary were an academic struggle. There were numerous failed papers and exams, and countless late nights memorizing flashcards for the Greek and Hebrew language tests. On a routine basis, I was forced to swallow my pride and throw myself on the mercy of Fuller's Access Services, a dedicated department formed to help students with special needs.

I GOT THAT ITCH

In October of 2013, I began a grueling new adventure. Waiting tables and leading youth retreats had grown stale. I needed a new challenge. My restless soul was thirsty for spiritual, intellectual, and theological stimulation. Instead of embarking on a six-month triathlon training program, I applied for the Doctorate of Ministry program offered by Fuller Seminary.

At the time that I applied for the Doctorate of Ministry program, I loved being a youth minister, but I longed for a spiritual recharge to remain faithful to my pastoral calling. I needed a group of peers to stimulate worn-out theology. I desired to have a deeper understanding and appreciation of the Christian faith. I sought further education to evolve as a spiritual leader and effective communicator, and to serve as a theological resource for the local community.

The program would fulfill my desire for professional development, but more than anything, I wanted to make a public statement to everyone who said I would be lucky to graduate high school or college. We can lose everything in this world, but no one can take away our memories, academic achievements, or faith in God.

THE PROCESS

Fuller's Doctorate of Ministry program is designed as a distance-learning program; students from across the globe are able to remain active in their current ministry while they are enrolled in the program. A large portion of studies are completed at home, but students must travel to California a few times a year to participate in Personalized Track courses, which are taught as one-week intensives. Numerous challenges arise as ministers try to balance life, ministry, and school. Fuller understands these challenges and gives students eight years to complete a three-year degree.

In February of 2014, our family drove 800 miles so I could participate in my first one-week intensive. Minutes after the Sunday evening service ended, Dodi and I loaded the toddlers into our beloved 2003 Toyota Sienna minivan. I suggested we drive all night so our young children could sleep for the majority of the 13-hour drive. For many solo travelers, a long drive across the beautiful Southwest is the perfect opportunity for personal reflection. When children are added to the desert oasis, a peaceful thirteen-hour car ride can quickly become a hellacious sixteen-hour nightmare.

To reach class on time, family members needed to sleep, be quiet, and hold their pee. We packed enough snacks to live underground for two years. Hunger or thirst would not derail this Pony Express. *The Mission of God in Local Contexts* was scheduled to begin at precisely 9 a.m. on Monday morning. And gosh darn it, I wasn't going to let crying, fighting, or dirty diapers stop this joy ride.

Jacked up on Monster Energy drinks and a delicate balance of turkey jerky, I rolled into class at 8:55. The moment I stepped onto campus, I knew it was a terrible decision to drive through the night. Sure, the drive saved our family hundreds of dollars, but tired angry theologians are the worst dads. On the bright side, our children do not remember this foolish decision.

I do not express immense gratitude when the alarm clock rudely ruins my beauty rest. Every morning is attacked with the proper amount of displeasure. No amount of caffeine could erase the fatigue from our treacherous all-night drive through the California desert.

At precisely 9:01 a.m., our instructor, Dr. Eric Jackson, welcomed students to the Doctorate of Ministry program. He took a few moments to share a brief personal introduction. He asked each student to introduce themselves to the class. A few of these brief introductions lasted well over fifteen minutes. Fifteen minutes is all the time I needed to bake a pizza or change the oil in the minivan. A brief introduction should last no longer than a minute. When it was my time to speak, my introduction lasted less than ten seconds. "My name is Andy Konigsmark. I live in Colorado. I'm a part-time youth minister and a part-time bartender. In my free time, I like to play games with our children."

With the not-so-brief introductions out of the way, Dr. Jackson asked, "Andy, of the assigned readings, which book spoke most to your current ministry situation?"

I could feel myself growing warm, and all eyes in the classroom became laser focused on the knowledge I was about to extoll upon my fellow classmates. Instead of wowing everyone, I sheepishly responded, "Well, this is embarrassing. I had no idea we were supposed to read ahead of time."

I would love to say we all had a little laugh about this misstep. Instead, Dr. Jackson asked to meet after class. Even in graduate school, it's never a step in the proper direction when you are summoned to the principal's office.

To say I was dressed down after class would be an understatement. Every fear and concern about school began to bubble up during the thirty-minute meeting. Dr. Jackson informed me

I was being placed on immediate academic probation. This was not the smooth start I was expecting on my first day of doctoral studies.

FOR THE NEXT PART

The first year of the doctoral program went rather smoothly after I learned the importance of thoroughly reading the syllabus. In the second year of the program, students form a thesis and proposal for their doctoral project. The project is designed to be a creative process, but it must serve as a practical response to each student's current ministry context. For example, a final project could create a church-sponsored after-school program to support single parents in their community. This particular project would address a specific need, and the results could be measured by parent and children involvement. This type of project would check all the required boxes.

In the second year of the doctoral program, I chose to participate in an independent study focusing on the art of storytelling to further my development as a writer and speaker. To receive credit for the course, I was required to read ten-thousand pages of approved reading material, write a fifty-page paper, and attend the National Storytelling Festival in Jonesborough, Tennessee. After completing all three components of course work, an assigned faculty member rewarded my efforts with a big fat zero. For someone struggling to complete a doctoral degree, zeros are not for heroes, and C's do not equal degrees.

With loads of grace, Dr. Jackson facilitated a three-month extension to rewrite the fifty-page paper. I was crushed by the failure but directed my time and energy to earn a passing grade. After carefully rereading the professor's comments regarding the failed project, I vigorously sought to correct all of the mistakes. I met with a local newspaper writer to create a new outline for the final draft. I paid an editor hundreds of dollars to review the final draft. Full of confidence, I turned in the over-hauled project. A few weeks later, I was informed for a second time that my fifty-page paper did not meet doctoral level requirements to receive a passing grade. In light of the circum-stances, I was mad, embarrassed, and distraught.

After the second failure, I seriously considered withdrawing from the Doctor of Ministry program. At the time, I was balancing ministry, the restaurant schedule, and raising young children. Life was more than full; I did not need the stress of school. Despite all of my diligence and hard work, I wasted close to a year of academic studies and over five-thousand dollars of school-related expenses.

To encourage growth and foster resilience, we must learn from our mistakes. From my perspective, this is much easier said than done. It is tough to learn from your mistakes when you're unable to comprehend the mistakes being made. In this particular moment of failure, I began to embrace an unfortu-nate reality; I graduated high school, college, and graduate school with the writing abilities of a middle school student. All I could do was make sure that this particular middle school student was cooler than a polar bear in a snowstorm and filled with Kanye West's self-confidence.

At this point in the doctoral program, I had two choices: quit or persevere. I chose to persevere and push through academic roadblocks. The path to the finish line would not be straight, but I would finish the race. We all face setbacks in life, but I embraced a new reality, "If earning an advanced degree is routine, the title of 'doctor' would not be worth the paper it's printed on."

FINISH LINE

At the beginning of 2017, the doctoral program's finish line was coming into view. Instead of landing with elegance, our immediate family was bracing for a crash landing. I'd completed all the required coursework, but the final project still loomed in the distance. Fuller Seminary requires all doctoral candidates to complete a final project. The ideal project addresses a specific need within the candidate's current ministry context.

As the project takes shape, an official proposal must be approved by the institution's doctoral review board. Once a project receives academic approval, students are given the green light to move forward. If a project is rejected, candidates must develop a different project that satisfies program requirements.

Fat Pitch, a screenplay about a minister willing to do anything to save his beloved church softball team, was the centerpiece of my original submission. Four weeks after submission, the review board harshly rejected the screenplay. The project was dismissed for numerous reasons. Most importantly, it did not address a current or felt need within our community.

I understand that a softball playing minister does not meet a specific need within in our community. But gosh darnit, I worked hard on this project. I received improper intel that the school would approve the project. *Fat Pitch* was a side project I started the year before I enrolled in the Doctorate of Ministry Program. When I first met with the school's program director, I shared my plan to submit a screenplay as the final project. Even before I returned to campus, the initial proposal was embraced with excitement. Fuller Seminary prides itself on a strong relationship with mainstream arts and culture.

Fat Pitch embarked on a four-year journey, which took place on long plane rides, late nights after the restaurant closed, and those precious moments when our children took long naps. In these uncertain years, the project survived numerous edits, rewrites, and rejections. When the dust settled, *Fat Pitch* was rejected by numerous screenplay festivals, writing collectives, producers, editors, agents, and finally Fuller Seminary. Countless time was invested into the screenplay, and now it was being left on the cutting room floor.

BREAKING BREAD

With *Fat Pitch* no longer a viable option, it was time to form a new plan. In December of 2017, full of hope and excitement, I submitted my final project titled *Breaking Bread: The Dynamic Relationship Between Bread and the Growing Post-Christian Movement in America*. Less than a month after submission, I received an email from the Program's Director. The message was clear—the final project was unacceptable. Over one hundred pages of *Breaking Bread* did not meet the program's strict degree requirements. The project was deemed to have the intellectual integrity of an eighth-grade project. At this level of penmanship, I should have included a menagerie of unsuitable potty humor.

I could not quit the program at this stage. Our family had invested too much time, energy, and resources. I was determined to prove everyone wrong. For the next three months, I drank more Red Bull than an X-Games athlete as I powered through late-night writing sessions. I paid professional editors and writers to examine and analyze the entire project. I asked friends, neighbors, and countrymen to proofread chapters from the project.

After a total overhaul of the final project and a thumbs-up from my editor, I resubmitted *Breaking Bread*. A few weeks later, I was horrified to learn the project had been deemed unacceptable for a second time! I could not believe the words I was reading, nor could I fathom the words I heard on a conference call with the program's director. "Andy, we see substantial improvement in your work, but your project falls noticeably short of our academic standards."

After *Breaking Bread* was rejected for a second time, I threw myself on the mercy of the program. I begged the school for any help they could offer. In April of 2018, the program facilitated a partnership with Doctor Lynn Moresi, a professor and lecturer of Christian studies. Dr. Moresi is not one to sugarcoat a bad situation.

"Andy, your paper is not commensurate with doctoral level work. We need to rewrite the majority of the paper. A few elements can be salvaged, but the rest is rubbish."

Even though I did not know the definition of "commensurate," Dr. Morosi pledged to guide *Breaking Bread* to the Promised Land—Oh, let manna fall from heaven—and lead me into a land filled with milk and honey. "Just tell me exactly what I need to do," I told her, "and I will do it."

For the next six months, I listened to every word, piece of advice, and scrap of instruction she offered. I could not accept the thought of my final project being rejected for a third time. Despite my rising anxiety levels, Dr. Morosi never wavered from her assurance. Every phone conversation was filled with assurance and a couple of four-letter words I dare not repeat. Together, we labored through a countless sequence of re-writes and edits. She was emphatic; if I followed her structure and guidance, the school would approve my final project.

With great apprehension, we resubmitted the project in November of 2018. A few weeks later, I received a short and simple email from Fuller Seminary. After a brief greeting, a bold line stated, "Your final project has been approved."

I thought, "Wait? What? Does this mean I passed the program? Does this mean I earned the title of doctorate?"

Instead of responding with an email, I called the school, seeking an explanation. The unemotional response was affirmative, "Andy, your final project has been approved. You met all of the requirements for Fuller's Doctor of Ministry program. Let me be the first to congratulate you, Doctor Konigsmark."

Initially, I could not comprehend the significance of the news I had received. The last five years had been filled with numerous failures and countless late nights. I could not believe I had completed all of the school's requirements. We had done it. Thanks to my sweet wife who encouraged me to endure, we had really done it. Thanks to my sweet mother who refused to take no for answer. Thanks to Fuller Seminary for not throwing out the baby with the bathwater. Thanks to Dr. Moresi, we crossed the finish line as promised. In December of 2018, with loads of support and encouragement, I officially earned a Doctorate of Ministry from Fuller Seminary.

LET'S CELEBRATE

To celebrate the momentous occasion, I did what anyone else would do, I hopped in the car and drove to work. It was more important than ever to clock in early to set up my tables for evening dinner service.

Most people celebrate the special moments in life with a glass of bubbly, a party, or dinner with a loved one. Armed with a fresh Doctorate of Ministry, I hopped into the mini-van and drove to work. Instead of personal celebration, I sold an expensive bottle of cabernet to table thirty-five. The young couple said they had come in for dinner to celebrate their engagement, but I couldn't be fooled. I knew they ordered that expensive bottle of wine for my special achievement. Thank you, random couple from Indiana for celebrating one of the greatest achievements of my personal life with me, even if you didn't know you did.

Despite my lofty goal to quit restaurant work, I still clock in three nights a week to support our family. Don't feel bad for me; feel bad for the customers who receive my divine servitude.

True, I have been defeated by the easy money of the restaurant industry, but I will not succumb to coworker pressure and purchase a metal crumber designed to sweep expensive bread-crumbs onto the floor. For now, I will continue to use my non-organic doctoral pinky finger to wipe vegan, organic, gluten-free, overpriced, non-GMO crumbs onto the floor. By the way, we charge extra for the steak sauce.

CHAPTER 20

DIVINE STRUGGLE

*"It ain't the parts of the Bible that I can't understand that bother me,
it's the parts that I do understand."*—Mark Twain

THE BIG WHY

Without question, I struggled through the academic process for over twenty-five years. Through all the lectures, tests, and final projects, I've learned one thing for sure—the more I study the nature of God, the less I pretend to understand it. There is not a single textbook, commentary, or author who can adequately dissect the mystery of God. If humans could comprehend the complex nature of God, then God would not be worthy to be called God.

As children, we do not have the tools to conceptualize the nature of God. For most, we experience the incomprehensible image of God while our little brains encounter the Tooth Fairy, Santa Claus, and pots of gold at the end of the rainbow. Children love the mystery of Christmas, the magic of the Tooth Fairy, and bunnies who deliver candy-filled baskets. As young brains form opinions about the world, eager minds are offered a jumbled mix of fairytale, magic, and religious instruction. As a result, countless children are left without a reliable guide as they explore the mystery of God.

Around age seven, our benevolent fairytales begin to present more questions than answers. For the first time, kids challenge the veracity of the Tooth Fairy, the trustworthiness of leprechauns, and the malevolent pirates who safeguard the treasure trove of boogers inside your nose. Unfortunately, the complex nature of God becomes a jumbled mess in this central time of self-exploration.

In these formative years, guiding children to an authentic experience with God becomes especially challenging when kids discover mom and dad lied about Rudolph the Red-Nosed Reindeer. The time to embrace youthful curiosity begins to take place when children forgive their parents for the salacious lies of Christmas past. As human beings contemplate the mystery of God, it remains imperative to embrace the unknown. As a faithful steward of God's infinite grace, I refuse to offer future generations empty platitudes, cheap clichés, or watered-down catchphrases to satisfy life's most difficult questions. Instead, I encourage inquisitive minds to ask the big questions as they embark on their unique spiritual journeys.

Our eight-year-old son loves to ask what happens when we die. Simultaneously, he is also curious about why the Incredible Hulk does not have a girlfriend. Unfortunately, I do not have great answers to either of these questions. I have several theories about the Incredible Hulk and his need for anger management, but these theories will not satisfy his curiosity. Instead of offering a watered-down response, I say, "Son, I've never been dead, so I don't know what happens when we die, but we can talk about what it means to live."

As a Christian minister, I believe we live to share the love of God. As global citizens, it's our mission to love our neighbor as we love ourselves. Before we can love our neighbor, we must know our neighbor. To know our neighbor, we must leave the Church and enter our local communities and simply ask, "What do you need?" When we ask this loaded question, we must be prepared to respond. These moments will move us outside of our comfort zones, but they will also create opportunities to build authentic relationships.

A SEARCH FOR ANSWERS

After years of study, I am confident of one thing: I don't have all the answers. Life would be much simpler if I could understand all the complexities of life, but there is so much I will never understand. I don't know why close to nine million people a year will die from hunger and hunger-related diseases. I don't know why evil people go unpunished. Yes, throughout history, dreadful acts have been performed or executed in the name of Jesus Christ. Yet, this is not the Jesus we encounter throughout Scripture. As a result of Christian injustice, millions of people around the world hate Jesus. But for many, including myself, Jesus and the Christian Church remain a source of hope, a sanctuary for restoration, and a pathway to the Divine mystery.

I remain rooted in my Christian faith because my life is captivated by the life and teachings of Jesus. Jesus entered our world, gathered His disciples, and began to establish God's sovereign nature. As children of God, we've been called to spread restorative love to a world full of broken, discarded, and abandoned individuals. The mission sounds implausible, but it will begin to grow as we plant seeds of boundless mercy, irresistible grace, and steadfast forgiveness.

To expand the unblemished love of God, Jesus calls His followers to eradicate poverty, fight injustice, and eliminate persecution. As we embrace the transcendent love of God, our hearts will swell with the spiritual awakening taking place within our souls. Through this purification process, our benevolent actions will be driven by generosity, servitude, and compassion.

IT'S NOT ABOUT GETTING INTO HEAVEN

To captivate our restless souls, Christianity must be more than salvation and free entrance to the pearly gates of Heaven. The Jesus we encounter in the Bible is more concerned about getting Heaven into us. He came into this world to teach us how to live. His earthly mission was filled with complex parables, audacious declarations, and a profound message of restoration. As a result, Jesus's followers are empowered to care for the oppressed, welcome the foreigner, and champion the marginalized.

As we draw towards the perfect love of God, our lives begin to fill with grace, forgiveness, and laughter. Let me say it again; it's not about getting into Heaven, but about getting Heaven into us. In a quest for spiritual fulfillment, we must create opportunities for the love of God to radiate through our lives. God's boundless love is shared through numerous avenues, including words of affection, acts of service, and even generous cash tips.

Adversaries will claim I am spreading liberal, progressive, hippy Christianity. Call it whatever you want, but Christianity is more than shame and guilt. Jesus did not expect perfection from his followers; instead, he sought discipleship. Pursuing the transformative grace of Jesus opens our lives to the God of wonders. Through this perfect love, I can establish Heaven in my life.

Why Didn't You Tell Me About Your Faith?

In the winter of 2009, a few days after performing at a local comedy festival, Jesse approached me at the gym. With a carefree stride, this young man strolled over to the bench press. Without missing a beat, he said, "My wife and I loved your performance the other night. Those jokes you did about growing up in Georgia hit a little close to home. I grew in South Georgia and moved to Colorado a couple of years after I graduated from college. How did you end up here?"

This simple conversation set the foundation for a lasting friendship. I often say, Jesse is everything I want to be when I grow up, except I am a few years older than him. Our friendship began with a visit to the gym and more weight loaded on the bench press than our little arms could handle. We found it necessary to skip the gym on glorious powder days on the mountain. There will always be more days to pump iron at the gym, besides we didn't move to Colorado to wear muscle shirts and strut like a peacock. No, Sir, the two of us moved to the Rocky Mountains in search of adventure. When summer rolled around, it was time to mount bikes and tackle the grueling uphill climbs our trails provide.

Two years after we began lifting weights together, Jesse asked, "Why haven't you told me about your faith?"

"Well, you never asked," I replied.

This simple question led to a spiritual awakening within Jesse's life. To explore our faith, we began to read the book, *Not Enough Faith to be an Atheist.* This book generated excellent conversations for the two of us. I have never loved to debate theology, but this was not a debate; it was the beginning of a spiritual journey. Despite being born in the Bible Belt and being surrounded by Christians most of his life, Jesse did not have a clear picture of the Christian faith. As a result, we embarked on a journey to explore Jesus.

A year after our intense study of the nature of God, the teachings of Jesus, and the wisdom of the Bible, Jesse said, "Hey man, I want to be a Christian." It is these moments that have drawn my life into ministry. Around age twenty-five, I began my long stumble into ministry. Becoming a member of the clergy has never been a haphazard decision, but being a minister was never my original plan. In my late teens, I wanted to be an auto-mechanic, and by the time I reached college, I was convinced I would become a marriage and family therapist. Yet, job opportunities outside the Church continued to close in my face. Meanwhile, the front doors of the Church called my name.

As a teenager, I discovered my heart was naturally drawn toward the community formed underneath the steeple. Years later, I enter the sacred space ready to share my God-given skills of comedy and storytelling. Before I step into the pulpit on Sunday morning, I spend hours crafting a sermon that drives to one applicable message. The message is formed around a central theme. Once the theme is identified, I stack layers of entry points on top of the message to engage the congregation. These layers include current events, personal stories, and funny anecdotes. Every part of the sermon is written with the congregation in mind. I want people to leave the service feeling encouraged, challenged, and motivated to respond to the call of God.

In addition to the joy I find through preaching, the baptism of both young and old breathes fire into my ministry. Over the course of my ministry, I've anointed the heads of innocent children, melted snow to fill the baptismal font, and dipped a best friend into a freezing river. In these beautiful moments, when we are surrounded by our loved ones, I'm given the honor of welcoming people into God's Royal Family. These moments are holy and set apart; I feel eternally grateful to the families who've invited me into this sacred space.

Jesus walked the earth two thousand years before I was born, but His message remains life-changing. On December 24, 1945, President Harry S. Truman addressed the nation with his annual Holiday Address. As millions of Americans gathered around their radios, Truman famously said, *"I do not believe there is one problem in this country or in the world today which could not be settled if approached through the teaching of the Sermon on the Mount."* The true message of Christianity is transformative, provocative, and maybe a bit scandalous. Religious opponents called Jesus a glutton, a drunkard, and a friend of tax collectors. I love everything about this Jesus, except overpaying on my federal taxes. Through God's work, I've nurtured transformative relationships through sports, comedy, and shots of tequila. In these sober spiritual awakenings, my soul is reminded of my initial call to ministry. Throughout my challenging spiritual journey, I've encountered numerous obstacles and received incredible blessings. A life worth living will be filled with challenges and opportunities; in turn, a journey of faith opens doors to an abundant life.

CHAPTER 21

WHAT'S IT ALL ABOUT?

"Everybody can be great...because anybody can serve. You don't have to have a college degree to serve. You don't have to make your subject and verb agree to serve. You only need a heart full of grace. A soul generated by love."—Martin Luther King

CHEATED

Recently, one of my best friends from childhood asked, "Andy, will you feel cheated if everything you believe is a lie? What if we die and there is no heaven? What if you spent all these years being a Christian only to find out it's a sham? Won't you feel cheated?"

I thought for a few seconds. "No, I won't feel cheated. I can't see any reason I will regret trying to make this world a better place."

His eyebrows raised. "Think about all the stuff you gave up."

"Exactly what did I give up?" I asked.

He thought for a moment. "The girls, the parties, and other stuff."

Unfortunately for many of us, we have been taught a very

limited view of God. As a teenager, I believed it. I proclaimed faith in Jesus Christ only because I was afraid of going to hell (the "fire insurance" I referred to earlier). I believed that as long as I professed Jesus Christ to be my Savior and was forgiven for my sins, I would be saved from eternal damnation and hellfire. Once I received my fire insurance, nothing could deny my entrance into the gates of heaven.

This weak and poor salvation theology causes people to set their eyes on the afterlife instead of focusing on establishing the love of God here on earth. As covered in the Gospels of Matthew, Mark, Luke, and John, Jesus invites the children of God to establish Divine love on earth. This establishment is known as the kingdom of heaven. In this kingdom, God's love is free to reign over the world.

Despite the teachings of Jesus, far too many evangelical Christians focus on eternal life. Our heads are stuck in heaven as we stumble around on the earth. Throughout the Bible's New Testament, Jesus does not focus on saving people from hell. He is fully aware of our ability to create hell on earth. Many of our friends, relatives and neighbors are currently living in their own painful version of hell. Do not lose heart. As we embrace God's limitless love, we can begin to destroy hell on earth.

WINNING THE LOTTERY

"Wouldn't it be amazing if I won the Mega-Millions jackpot in the lottery?" I said to my mother one evening. "The jackpot is going to be over one billion this weekend. One billion dollars! I could give everyone in the family at least fifty million, we could give World Vision over a hundred million, and there would still be money left over. I could buy a '69 Camaro. Mom, we would never have to worry about money again. You could buy a second home in Hawaii."

This Wise Owl known as my mother said, "Andy, it would be

awful to win all that money. With that much money, you would never experience the joy of saving every penny to buy your first home. When you're living paycheck-to-paycheck, the lottery sounds like the answer to all your problems, but it's the struggle that makes life great."

In the midst of struggle, nothing feels great. No one wants to hear, "God must be trying to teach you a lesson." For instance, when I tore the anterior cruciate ligament in my knee for a fourth time at the age of thirty-four, I was not rushing to worship service on Sunday mornings to praise God. To place this injury into perspective, fifty-one National Football League players tore their ACL's in 2017. This number accounts for less than three percent of all NFL players. Tearing an ACL for a second time is not uncommon for competitive athletes, but suffering the injury four times is a statistical anomaly, according to our local orthopedic surgeon.

This injury did not feel like a blessing the first, second or third time, let alone the fourth. My initial reaction was, "Why, God? Why me? I take great care of my body. I eat right. I exercise daily. I am faithful. Oh Lord, you know I try to be faithful. I don't deserve this. I don't smoke cigarettes. I don't drink alcohol. Well, maybe I occasionally have a little tequila, but it's just a little bit. You know I'm nice to my mama. Is asking for one healthy knee too much?"

While playing basketball with a group of high school kids, I heard a sudden and familiar popping sound and immediately knew surgery would be needed to repair the ligament. Limping home from the basketball gym, a deep physical and emotional struggle began to form. In short order, hospitals, doctors, and physical therapists would begin mailing exorbitant medical bills to the house. From prior experience, surgery and recovery would be painful. After being released from the hospital, I was still facing six months of intense physical rehab and doctor approval before resuming normal activities.

Despite the physical setback, I refused to let one more injury steal my joy for outdoor recreation. During the six months of rehab, I vowed to restore my body to full health. I would not let this injury or previous surgeries deter my sense of adventure. These surgically-repaired knees would return to fight another day.

Six years after surgery, I share my story to encourage those facing a major knee surgery for the first time. I learned to snowboard after tearing my ACL the first time. Three years after my second ACL reconstruction, I made it to the semi-finals of the new *American Gladiators* with Hulk Hogan. A month after my third ACL reconstruction, I spent six weeks back-packing across Europe. Two years after tearing my ACL for the fourth time, I was able to compete on *American Ninja Warrior*. Thanks to God and unwavering family support, these knobby, surgically-scarred knees have carried my body thousands of miles, climbed 14,000 feet to help me witness beautiful sunsets, and crossed enough finish lines to stoke the competitive fires for years to come. I still don't enjoy the struggle, but I hope my struggle will serve as an inspiration to others.

Despite the numerous injuries and medical bills, I refuse to quit. I only have one body to experience the world with, and I plan on getting my money's worth. I hate being injured but feel blessed to serve as an inspiration for those who are in the midst of pain and suffering. No one wants to struggle, but the struggle promotes the greatest opportunities for growth.

Best-selling author, TED speaker, and research professor Brene Brown proclaims, "You're imperfect, and you're wired for struggle, but you are worthy of love and belonging."

Every single person encounters different struggles; they are a natural state of affairs. Great leaders, transcendent athletes, and talented performers experience setbacks and heartbreak. Personal struggles do not suggest a life spiraling out of control. On the contrary, a beautiful and fulfilling life will present challenges. How we embrace the challenge or struggle will define the quality and outcome of our lives.

WHAT DOES GOD HAVE TO SAY?

As long as humans inhabit the earth, life will be filled with an ongoing struggle to embrace a world filled with pain, evil and suffering. In 2017, The Federal Bureau of Investigation reported over 17,000 murders in America. Based on these numbers, 47 Americans are murdered every day. That's two people every hour, or one person every thirty-two minutes. However, the violent nature of human beings cannot be blamed for all of life's problems.

Humans are causing dangerous environmental ripple effects through pollution, overpopulation, deforestation, and over-farming. According to research by the World Health Organization, 5.6 million children under the age of five died from malnutrition in 2016. Based on the current research, 15,000 children will die every day simply because they do not have enough food to survive. Natural disasters kill 90,000 people per year and affect the lives of 160 million people worldwide.

As the world continues to advance, science and technology bring the human story to light. When science cannot provide answers, people look to the Divine to answer life's most difficult questions. Despite calling on the power of the Almighty, an absence of satisfying answers sweeps over the community when a three-year-old girl is diagnosed with terminal cancer. There is nothing righteous or holy about watching an innocent child suffer.

Life is messy. Religion can be painful. Faith is an ongoing exercise in perseverance. Belief in God is a willful recognition of humility. The Almighty can never be fully known. Those who are drawn into deep connection with the Divine will be humbled by the incomprehensible nature of God. Despite our best efforts to acquire ultimate knowledge, there will always be more to learn. With ultimate knowledge comes complete power. With absolute power, humans would discard religion, faith, and God. Much to our chagrin, we cannot control every facet of life. Humans do not have all the answers. We do not have absolute power to control every aspect of our existence. Despite unexpected trials and tribulations, however, humans do possess complete control over our responses to any given circumstance. Through the Divine, we can embrace a transcendent spiritual journey which provides total freedom to respond to the roller coaster of life. As autonomous beings, it is our decision to embrace an all-loving God or blame the universe for all of our problems.

HOW DO WE RESPOND TO STRUGGLES?

While writing this chapter, I was diagnosed with a wicked viral infection called shingles. To explain the pain, imagine lighting poison ivy on fire and then rubbing the hot coals on your body. The pain is not quite that bad, but it's pretty close. For those who are unfamiliar, shingles is the adult version of chicken pox. Your nervous system is being attacked by the virus, and a simple task such as getting dressed or a shower can lead to unbearable pain. Your skin is covered in painful welts; yet the virus is called shingles. A better name might be Horse Warts or Fire Puss. No one has respect for a disease called shingles. Just imagine for a second if chicken pox were called bricks; no one would care about your symptoms.

Throughout life, physical setbacks serve as a reminder that few things in life are certain. A life well-lived will include death, taxes, and personal struggles. In the midst of struggle, it's imperative to focus on our abilities, not disabilities. As students, we can call teachers incompetent, or we can put in extra work to rise to the top. On the baseball field, we can blame the coach for not giving us a chance to play, or spend extra time honing our strengths and improving upon our weaknesses. In marriage, we can point to the perceived shortcomings of our partner, or we can focus on offering the best version of ourselves. In an effort to live an abundant life, we must focus on possibilities rather than problems.

Humans are marvelous creatures blessed with the unique ability to infuse life with purpose. In the midst of struggle, we must stop playing the role of a victim whose life is fraught with insurmountable problems. We do not have to be defined by our shortcomings. Instead, we can use personal challenges to fuel and propel our future success. Life will knock us down, but it's how many times we get back up that makes the difference.

SHARING THE STRUGGLE

As the Information Age grows, evolves and dominates all facets of society, the American Dream has become a flawed reality. Facebook, Instagram and Twitter are ideal platforms for sharing life's idyllic moments. It has been said that a picture says a thousand words, but we are controlling the flow of information with the pictures we choose to share. With zero hesitation, we grab our phones to share pictures of a once-in-a-lifetime vacation to Tahiti. We log on to post pictures of our beautiful children, romantic dinners, and fun nights with friends. We grant the world unlimited access to view our amazing accomplishments. Celebrating life is not a crime, but we tend to hide the moments that lack sparkle and shine.

Despite living in a world with unlimited connection, more people are feeling lonelier than ever. The social media façade is just one of the reasons Americans are feeling disconnected. The Internet works as a powerful anti-depressant, offering instant personal feedback on life's accomplishments. We grab the keyboard to proudly share life's best moments, while simultaneously hiding personal struggles. American culture says, "It's okay to brag about life, as long as you hide your problems." Friends are quick to divulge details about the kitchen remodel, but slow to disclose marriage difficulties. The cultural phenomenon known as social media promotes sharing the best moments of life while systematically disassembling the cultural safety nets which cradle our personal struggles.

In an effort to protect our image, we downplay our failures, hide our fears, and project a magnificent life. By adulthood, we have mastered the ability to pretend everything is perfect. Fearing rejection, we hide our insecurities and bury our failures. Self-preservation teaches us to build walls around personal struggles. These mighty walls promote privacy and control the flow of information. Unfortunately, these social walls also deny friends, family and neighbors the opportunity to learn from our struggles.

Fearing rejection, we only allow the world to view the best versions of ourselves. We flaunt our strengths and hide our weaknesses. Instead of embracing our perceived flaws, we hide problems from the scrutiny of the outside world. To flourish in the Information Age, we must cast aside the unwritten social media rules and stop pretending everything is perfect. Life is messy, and that's okay. Forget the unspoken rules and begin embracing the struggle we call life. Jesus was the master of embracing the struggle. Christian or not, lives flourish in the face of authenticity.

COMEDY IS A STRUGGLE

Despite the allure of bright lights, dark clubs, and supportive laughter, I found myself being pulled toward ministry, outdoor recreation, and family life. At thirty years old, I was incapable of having it all. If I were twenty-two years old and had little desire to be married, the story might have turned out differently. I love performing on the big stage, but delivering finely rehearsed punchlines is not my reason for being.

Ten years after being called into ministry, stand-up has become a hobby, not a way of life. Life as a minister continues to serve as a blessing as it creates plenty of space to attend birthdays, recitals, and soccer games. Despite years of balancing multiple part-time jobs, I have plenty of time to focus on my reason for being—a deep desire to be a devoted husband and father. Snowboarding, mountain biking, and adventure-racing serve as a life source. A great year is measured by outdoor adventure, family vacations, and uncontrollable fits of laughter. Even without earning a steady paycheck as a comedian, my life feels full. My family and I are chasing adventure and joy, not financial success or positions of status.

As a stand-up comic, I love to share my stories of struggle. Armed with only a microphone, I share the most painful moments of life with complete strangers. I invite audiences to laugh at my stupid mistakes, painful memories, and memorable shortcomings. These performances are cathartic moments that steal power from the most painful situations I have encountered. Over the years, I have told jokes about my learning disabilities, battles with depression, the pitfalls of being a server, shortcomings as a father, and the numerous mistakes I have made as a minister. I do not pretend to have it all together, and I'm okay with that.

Sharing our personal stories of struggle is one of the most powerful ways to build our sphere of influence. The world is drawn to humility, not arrogance. In fact, while the Apostle Paul was shackled in jail, he told a group of early Christians in Philippi, "Do nothing out of selfish ambition or vain conceit. Rather, in humility, value others above yourselves, not looking to your own interests but each of you to the interests of the others. (Philippians 2:3-4)." Humans grow tired of the person who remains the hero of every story. Instead, audiences of all ages build an immediate connection with the tragically flawed underdog. It is far easier to identify with stories of pain and suffering than moments of majestic greatness. Not everyone is called to be a minister or stand-up comedian. We do not need a stage or pulpit to share our stories of adversity. The mere willingness to share the struggle will fortify our resolve. For everyone willing to listen, perseverance in the face of adversity will produce wisdom worthy to be shared with our community. To leave a mark on this world, it is imperative to accept failure. Sharing our stories of struggle is an excellent way to capture the hearts of the audience.

Remember, Thomas Edison tried thousands of versions of the light bulb before discovering the one that worked. He could have thrown up his hands and quit at any point, but he didn't. He failed upward. He learned from every setback and did things differently the next time. He persevered until he was victorious. And he didn't stop at the light bulb, either. Edison's inventions include the phonograph, the motion picture camera, and the tattoo pen. In all, he had 512 invention patents. He refused to let failure stand in his way; he trusted his ability to create the first sustainable lightbulb. Despite numerous setbacks and failures, he remained focused on the task at hand.

True leaders display courage when faced with adversity. Instead of throwing in the towel, they search for new ways to confront their problems. Edison's inventions changed the landscape of the modern world, but his perseverance in the face of adversity was what truly made him a world-changer. His words are as true today as they were in his lifetime—"Our greatest weakness lies in giving up. The most certain way to succeed is always to try just one more time."

THERE IS NO CHURCH GUILT

The church does not always point to the grace of God as we struggle with our spiritual journey. In childhood, our church propagated copious amounts of guilt about alcohol, sex, money, and church attendance. When the senior pastor says, "I've noticed y'all haven't been at church lately," he's not looking for more money in the donation basket. (Well, maybe that too.) Instead, it has been my experience that the local minister believes our holiness is directly tied to church attendance. In this limited theology, those with perfect attendance will enter the Pearly Gates of Heaven. For Christians in the American South, there was always tremendous amounts of guilt associated with church attendance. This guilt-based relationship creates a false paradigm in our relationship with God. Jesus came to the world to establish love and restoration, not guilt. A quest for peace and gratitude should be more than enough to fill the church on Sunday morning.

In closing, this book is not intended to attack my conservative Christian childhood. I was raised by two loving parents who provided more than enough adoration, compassion, and resources for my family. Additionally, I am no longer trying to repress my born-again teenage years. I fondly recall Sunday night youth group being one of my favorite nights of the week. Neither is it my intention to criticize my evangelical peers. I understand some people will argue that I have walked away from the core of the Christian faith. Instead, I believe I am walking into a deeper relationship with God. Together, we will view my spiritual journey in light of painful human struggles.

During my years serving as an ordained minister and bartender, I have listened to countless stories about spiritual wounds my friends suffered at the hands of the church. The most powerful moments revolved around gender and sexuality. I was raised in a tradition where the spouse was expected to be submissive to her husband in all areas of life. Our Baptist church taught that abstinence is the only way to remain sexually pure in God's eyes. From the pulpit, abortion was regularly referred to as murder. We were told that gays and lesbians were an abomination to God.

Christians within our Southern Baptist community worked tirelessly to stop schools from teaching students about safe sex. They launched powerful political campaigns to stop same-sex marriage. I can recall painful stories of parents and families rejecting their sons and daughters for becoming members of the LGBTQ community. This destructive theology is pushing people further away from the love of Jesus. Far too many denominations within the Christian tradition are morphing into a regimen of behavior control. When Christians focus on behavior, we begin walking away from the love of God.

As a minister, I encounter far too many people who've been hurt by the church. Most individuals can point to a specific moment or church scandal that instilled painful memories. As we know, the church does not have the power to hurt anyone. Broken people trying to control their world become the most dangerous perpetrators of painful church experiences.

As with most Christians, I have endured painful church memories. However, my experiences did not discourage my spiritual trajectory. This may sound petty, but sometimes, I wished the overweight music minister would have been caught having an affair with the church janitor. Or the leader of the high school Bible Society would have been caught taking money from the collection plate. I would have settled for the crusty church founder who couldn't believe I would defile the sanctuary with blue jeans getting caught visiting a bordello. This would have added some much-needed spice to our overly-evangelical Sunday morning worship services.

The truth is I do not carry permanent emotional scars from Sunday school or youth group. Even my ultra-conservative, ropes course-loving youth pastor deserves a fair amount of grace. With his limited training and education, the poor guy was desperately trying to instill Christian values into a group of sexually-repressed teenagers.

If we are truly faithful followers of Jesus, we must create a safe space to address doubt. Without asking questions, our faith will become weak and shallow. One of Jesus's most trusted companions is remembered as Doubting Thomas. After Jesus's death and resurrection, Thomas began asking questions. He is not applauded for seeking truth. No one calls him Analytical Thomas or Forward-Thinking Thomas. Instead, he is remembered for his doubt, despite the fact that he died professing his eternal love for Jesus.

CUDDLE DOES NOT RHYME WITH STRUGGLE

Our son, Crew, was introduced to life's adversity within minutes after being born. As the doctors brought him into this world, it was apparent his lungs had not fully developed in the womb. For the next couple of weeks, oxygen was pumped into his nose to protect his little body. From the day he entered this world, no one promised him a life free from struggle.

Our son's story reminds all of us that life is full of challenges. However, we do not need to be defined by them. Instead, we have the ability to overcome and share our struggle with others. Our willingness to share the most painful moments of life will give others the strength to persevere.

For many, the difference between success and failure is quite small. In the midst of struggle, we have two options: use the struggle to fuel our passions or allow the struggle to serve as an excuse for our problems. Humans have been blessed with the Divine ability to rise above their struggles. To excel, use your struggles to define who you want to become.

With a resume that includes a Bachelor's in Psychology, a

Master of Divinity, and Doctorate of Ministry, I have more degrees than a burnt piece of chicken. Yet, possessing a formal education is not enough. To evolve, we must seek avenues for growth. Yes, we might fail. We may bomb on stage in front of millions of people. We may miss the game-tying free throw. But embracing the struggle will foster more opportunities for growth. I've needed to struggle so I could grow as a comedian, athlete, father, husband, coworker, friend, sibling, and minister.

Remember, your personal story is powerful. Do not be afraid to show the world the cracks in your façade. As we embrace failure, we open ourselves to greater opportunities. At this moment, a close friend may be experiencing the same struggle you encountered last year. By sharing your story, you could provide that friend or neighbor with the skills, wisdom, and inspiration to learn a valuable lesson. Heroes come in all shapes, sizes, and demographics. Your story might be the spark someone needs to regain control of their life. Tomorrow, a new adventure awaits, and you have the ability to embrace the struggle that makes life beautiful.

KEEP IN MIND

Humans are biologically wired to seek answers to life's most difficult questions. Faith starts to crumble when we stop searching for the deeper meaning. Spiritual leaders become dangerous when followers believe their leader has all the answers. Throughout the Gospels, Jesus responds to questions by asking his own question or by responding with a parable. Jesus's thought-provoking questions and parables were offered to create entry points for understanding. The Son of God could have provided a straightforward answer, but he knew answering the questions would only create more problems.

We can argue 'till we are blue in the face about the nature of Jesus. We are free to debate the creation of the world. We can attack the actions of Christian extremists, but I will stop offering faith-based answers to faith-based questions. Before I am written off as a heretic, I firmly believe Jesus is calling us toward a personal resurrection. Many individuals are struggling to face tomorrow because their lives are being torn apart by fear, apathy, and abuse. Yet Jesus's life and death proclaim the power of a personal resurrection. God wants the children of earth to restore the world to something beautiful—a flawless world that exists under the reign of God's immeasurable love. We have the opportunity to embrace a personal resurrection to rise to something greater.

THE BUTTERFLY

I would be remis remind everyone, that I was a rowdy child always in search of mischief. It was a spirited childhood covered with a dog suit and flea bites. The summer before kindergarten was filled with water balloon wars, mud pies, and the eternal quest to discover treasure. This quest was challenged by persistent humidity, copperhead snakes, and an insidious battle with poison ivy.

One afternoon, I came running in the house yelling, "Mom! Mom! Look what I found!" I wasn't quite sure what I'd found.

With sweetness in her voice, she said, "Oh honey, that's a cocoon. Pretty soon, a butterfly will emerge from it."

"Please Mom, can we keep it? Please say yes? Just let me keep it for a little while."

My mother said, "Honey, go grab the old aquarium, and we'll place some sticks and leaves on the bottom. We can string a light over the aquarium, and we'll wait for it to hatch."

In the mind of a five-year-old boy, the butterfly was going to obliterate the cocoon in a matter of minutes. We put the cocoon inside the aquarium, and I began to wait. An hour later, nothing had happened. Another hour passed and still nothing happened.

Friday came and went. This lazy butterfly needed to get on with this cocoon business and do some stuff. Early Saturday morning, I noticed the butterfly beginning to push through the cocoon. I sat there transfixed as its wings began to poke through the bottom of the cocoon. I watched as the butterfly struggled to free itself.

It was a hopeless moment as I watched the butterfly struggle. I couldn't just sit there and watch; I had to help. I ran to the kitchen to grab a pair of scissors. Without hesitation or obedience, I sprinted full speed to my room with the scissors. It was time to abandon the rules. There was a life at stake in room five. Our local patient was unable to free itself from the insidious death clutch of its cocoon. I thought I had to use the scissors to free the helpless creature. The world moved into slow-motion. The butterfly tumbled toward the bottom of the aquarium. I watched as it hobbled around with its swollen and misshapen body.

I thought, "Oh no, it's sick." I ran to find my mother. "Mom, mom, the butterfly came out of the cocoon, and it doesn't look good. It looks sick. Something's wrong with it. It can't fly. Something is wrong."

My mom entered my room and noticed the pitiful butterfly, "Oh honey, did you use those scissors to help the butterfly?"

"Mom, it was stuck. I couldn't let it die."

She took a moment to gather her thoughts. "Honey, a butterfly must struggle to free itself from the cocoon. The physical struggle prepares this beautiful creature for a new life."

"No, Mom, you don't understand. If I didn't help, it was going to die. I couldn't let my butterfly die."

"Sweetie, now this poor butterfly doesn't chance to survive on its own. It's hard to believe, but it physically needed to struggle in the cocoon to prepare its body for the outside world." Our lives are akin to the metamorphosis of the butterfly. In the struggle, we develop a true sense of beauty. The struggle gives us strength, resolve, and compassion for a broken world. Struggle doesn't feel good in the midst of darkness. Yet, it's in the darkest hour that we open ourselves up to greater possibilities, opportunities, and moments to shine. Sometimes in life, we've got to push ourselves through the tiny hole in the cocoon so we can ascend to something greater. Grab hold of the rope, embrace the struggle, and remain open to life.

NOTES

17. EXPERIENCE CHANGES EVERYTHING

1. Stanley Hauerwas, *Matthew* (Brazos Theological Commentary on the Bible; Grand Rapids: Brazos Press, 2006), 211.

Made in the USA
Monee, IL
04 October 2020

43648939R10135